Animation

2D and beyond

RotoVision

Animation

2D and beyond

Jayne Pilling

A RotoVision Book
Published and distributed by
RotoVision SA
Rue du Bugnon 7, CH-1299
Crans-Près-Céligny, Switzerland

RotoVision SA
Sales & Production Office
Sheridan House
112/116A Western Road, Hove
East Sussex BN3 1DD, UK

T: +44 (0)1273 727 268
F: +44 (0)1273 727 269
sales@rotovision.com
www.rotovision.com

10 9 8 7 6 5 4 3 2 1

ISBN 2-88046-445-5

Book design by Opera Design
(Breda, The Netherlands)

Production and separation by
ProVision Pte. Ltd., Singapore
T: +65 334 7720
F: +65 334 7721

Contents

Introduction

Over the last century, traditional 2D animation has dominated commercial animation production, yet the use of new computer technologies now challenges the formerly rigid distinctions between 2D and 3D in terms of both the production and post-production processes. Such growing hybridisation meant it was more apt to title this book Animation 2D and beyond, whilst maintaining an emphasis on the drawn.

In the last 30 years the huge explosion in all kinds of animation being produced around the world has led to a far greater diversity of style, technique and content. Although children's entertainment remains the industry's commercial backbone, new outlets for animation have emerged, appealing to a far wider age range. State deregulation of television in the West has led to a proliferation of new channels, many catering for niche audiences, and this has increased the demand for animation in all its forms. More animation is seen than ever before, including that used on CD Rom and video games, and movie special effects.

International festivals are another factor in raising the profile of animation, and have mushroomed all over the world, reflecting growing audience interest. Short films are the lifeblood of such festivals. Since most animation is extremely labour-intensive, shorts are often seen as the 'research and development' branch of the industry; a test-bed for new ideas, approaches, styles and techniques.

For many filmmakers, and audiences, animated shorts are also an end in themselves, and for some they are an art form with its own aesthetic. Free of the constraints of cinematic photo-realism, animation offers unlimited imaginative scope, particularly for personal expression. The magic of seeing and believing something unimaginable is clearly a source of audience fascination. It comes as no surprise that many animators were keen amateur magicians as children.

For many, short form personal animation is attractive for the degree of individual input and control it allows, and the fact it can be done almost single-handed, or with a very small team. Such films are often made in ways quite unlike the standardised industrial production model, which requires large numbers of people, a high degree of division of labour and specialised craft skills, and enormous amounts of advance planning and organisation. Although some animators making personal films set themselves technical and expressive challenges which demand

equally high levels of logistical complexity, the difference is that they can call the shots.

The process of making traditional, drawn animation is now fairly well-known – all the more so as every major animated feature release tends to be accompanied by a book or TV documentary detailing how the feature was made. This book concentrates largely, but not exclusively, on auteur animation, which allows us to give a taste of the diversity mentioned above.

The book is neither a 'how-to' manual nor a work of critical analysis. The aim is to give an insight into the creative process across a diverse range of animation filmmakers, focusing on a small number of different films or projects they have made.

Although the process of animation is the book's main focus, the circumstances under which films are made clearly impinge upon, and indeed can condition, the process itself. Developments in animation production worldwide have seen changes, not unlike those in live-action cinema, where distinctions between 'commercial' and 'independent' films no longer necessarily signal 'mainstream' or 'oppositional'. Major Hollywood studios regularly attend festivals to scout new talent, whilst the Aardman Studio is the most obvious example of how short, personal filmmaking can lead to major commercial success. Nick Park's films featuring the characters Wallace and Gromit not only brought in finance for the feature film **Chicken Run**, but also prompted British TV to realise there was an audience for animation that went beyond children. This led, for example, to the TV special, **Flatworld**, by Daniel Greaves, whose previous Oscar-winning short was made after hours, once he'd done a day's work animating commercials.

Selecting a range of diverse, internationally acclaimed animator-directors from an initial list of over 50 filmmakers, working exclusively or mainly in 2D, initially seemed an impossible task. However, the book was not intended to be a comprehensive survey of the entire 2D field, nor a critical ranking exercise. The requirement for maximum stylistic diversity across a filmmaker's work, and a preference for those who have used a range of different techniques, militated, sadly, against those acknowledged masters such as Joanna Quinn or Paul Driessen, whose work is instantly recognisable in every frame.

Personal animation is one of the few areas of filmmaking in which, since the '70s, women have made as strong a contribution as men. The selection here simply reflects the inevitable constraints of schedule, budget and animators' availability. Sometimes, although the animator might have been available, visual production material wasn't: not only because few people can store the vast amount of artwork generated, but also because some don't keep it – being more interested in moving on to the next project. Some filmmakers' peripatetic working lives have left material scattered around the globe.

It also seemed worth considering diversity not only in terms of approach, visual style and geography, but also in terms of production context. Making a living purely from short films is rarely possible, given the unfeasible economics of exhibition and distribution. Some countries offer relatively generous public funding for shorts, hence animator Gil Alkabetz' move to Germany, since there were no such opportunities in his native Israel. The Canadian National Film Board has long supported personal filmmaking. Wendy Tilby cites their 'faith and patience' over the four years her project took to make – beginning as a one page treatment, having visuals that changed enormously over the film's evolution, and never having a proper storyboard. This constancy was rewarded with the film's multiple awards.

International translocation is a fact of life for many animators. Post-Perestroika, state funding for animation in the ex-Soviet Union and Eastern Europe has declined dramatically. Estonian cultural pride at regaining independence has supported animation there, but its leading director Priit Pärn also derives income from regular teaching stints in Finland and his work as an artist. Igor Kovalyov moved from Russia to the highly successful American studio Klasky Csupo, which supports his own, quite uncommercial filmmaking in exchange for his input to their innovative features and TV series production such as **RugRats**. French studio Folimage enables young European animators to make a short there, alongside the studio's commercial productions. Their recently established European animation school is symptomatic of the way the industry's global growth has increased the number of training courses around the world, consequently providing employment for visiting animators as teachers. Some enjoy teaching for the contact with young, developing filmmakers as there are spin-off cultural exchange benefits and networking opportunities to be had, and some prefer to teach rather than freelance on the studio 'factory line'.

A desire to explore the American studio system led Piet Kroon to leave his native Holland for the West Coast. While there he also directed a personal film, financed as an Anglo-Dutch co-production, working with teams of animators in various parts of Europe. Co-production is a necessity for high budget TV half-hours or features in Europe, as Michel Ocelot discovered when he embarked on his first feature film. His 'overnight success', he observes wryly, took many years of frugal living, and his survival as a filmmaker could never have supported a family. Ocelot had never wanted to freelance on commercial productions such as television specials, which is how British filmmakers Mark Baker and Neville Astley came to meet, and went on to form a partnership.

Astley-Baker's move into series production highlights both a pragmatic strategy to generate commercial work they find congenial, but also how, over time, some animators find the attraction of 'doing it all yourself' – can pall. Although, as Baker observes, 'in a way it's against an animator's nature to direct, you'd rather take it away and do it all yourself', they have discovered the benefits of the enormous increase in productivity, which results from working with the much larger team a series requires. This size of team demands a greater degree of organisation and Baker finds the discipline implicit in this quite useful. 'Most people go into animation because they have a visual idea they want to see on screen and quite often all the preparatory stages seem boring, laborious and very restricting. If you have to stick to a written script, you worry: what if you have a better idea later? But often you don't. As each production stage involves solving different problems, that means when you're animating you don't worry about the story, you worry about details of the animation. So, you're on safer ground if it's all been worked out in advance, you can relax and trust it's going to work as a story.'

Such an approach is in marked contrast to that of Lejf Marcussen, for whom every film has to be a process of discovery, including that of where the film actually begins. He is driven to create resolutely non-verbal, non-narrative films, and his refusal to submit the script or treatment usually required makes fundraising difficult. He prefers to work virtually single-handed, like many other strongly art-oriented animators, and sees using computers as his way forward.

Commercials offer another working option, as animators with a highly individualistic style often appeal to advertising agencies. Their high budgets can offer opportunities to experiment, under pressure that is different from that of more personal work. Philip Hunt has taken this route, and his chapter also reminds us that animation is rarely the work of only one individual.

Along with Jean-Loup Felicioli, Neville Astley and Daniel Greaves, Philip Hunt has worked in both model and drawn animation, whereas others, such as Alkabetz, feel strongly committed to 2D. Mixing media is a hallmark of Simon Pummell's films, which some might argue are not animation at all. In the UK in particular, through Channel 4, and to a much lesser degree elsewhere in Europe, TV fully or partially funds animated shorts, which is how Pummell has been financed, along with a public arts subsidy designed to encourage artists to work with new technologies.

Shifting focus to a purely commercial production context, John Cary Films' revival of the cult TV series, **Captain Pugwash**, highlights the tendency of much children's animation to be producer-led, as was, for example, the classic John Coates' production **The Snowman**.

Japan has a huge 2D animation industry, and there's little opportunity for work outside that of TV series, features and pop promos. Yet it is clear (though perhaps less so to Western viewers) that it allows for enormous imaginative scope and a personal stamp, as with the work of Koji Morimoto.

Whatever the working context, temperament and motivation remain deeply personal, and highly variable from individual to individual. Each chapter is based on an interview with each contributor, and this format is designed to retain as much of these individual voices as possible. The materials gathered were often rich and interesting enough to warrant an entire book, rather than a single chapter, compounding the obvious frustration that the printed page can never convey the full magic of the moving image, nor compensate for the lack of its accompanying soundtrack.

I hope however that all the time and effort so generously contributed by each of the featured filmmakers gives some sense of just a fraction of their works' fascination, and the fabulous diversity within 2D animation.

In addition to all the contributors, other thanks, besides the acknowledgements made elsewhere are also due: to those guardians of the Estonian animation heritage, the unholy triumvirate of festival directors Gerben Schirmer (Holland), Chris Robinson (Canada) and Otto Alder (everywhere) for their generous loan of visual materials; to Chris O'Reilly, Charlotte Lambert, Julia Parfitt, Shigeto Samaya at Nexus; to animator and art director Gill Bradley, and to producer Ian McCue for their patient explanations and accumulated knowledge; to all at Varga London for their support and to Alex Jennings for Photoshop tuition; and John Cary for his glossary. My assistant Laura Meecham deserves a special mention and heartfelt gratitude, for her hard work, unfailing support and simply being herself. For their encouragement, listening and advice, producer Dick Arnall and Israeli animation specialist, Tsvika Oren, thank you. Finally, due credit should go to Kate Noël-Paton, my editor at RotoVision, who came up with the idea for this series, and is responsible for the format and overall look of the book.

Neville Astley and Mark Baker

From shorts to series production

Mark Baker and Neville Astley seem to have achieved the rare feat of moving from short, personal filmmaking to TV series on their own terms, despite or perhaps because of their rather unconventional approach. Having set up a studio in 1994 intending to combine making short films with commercials, they found that the two things don't slot that neatly together. Waiting for the phone to ring hoping a job will come in, can foster frustration rather than creativity. Baker comments, 'It's simply not worth spending so much of your life producing so little material. In 18 months we've produced more for the series than we have in our combined careers to date; and we want to make our living as animation filmmakers. Whether it's a film or a series, the starting point is the same: you think of ideas. Although, whereas a short must be complete in itself, with a series the story never ends, it's more to do with situations and characters.'

They didn't want a domestic set-up, but one in which the protagonists 'went out and did things... a structure within which we can be inventive'. Initially they avoided revisiting Baker's graduation film, **The Three Knights**, 'but what's good about **Knights** is it's obvious what they do and they're potentially quite funny. I loved Monty Python's 'Holy Grail' mix of heroism and absurdity. And the idea of giving them pets, also dressed in heavy armour, sealed it.'

Given the budget and schedule constraints of series production, compared to those of short films, they wanted to find a way to make the series themselves, rather than sending the animation abroad as is usual to reduce costs. 'We couldn't think beyond trying to simplify the techniques we knew – drawing every frame on paper, tracing and putting on cel. It took a while to make the leap to the computer animation technique we finally devised.' As the project was initially a shot in the dark, and the full pilot episode usually required by broadcasters would need a full script – 'when we didn't yet know the characters well enough', they felt a two-minute trailer could test the water and be developed according to response. It could also 'demonstrate things which might not come across on the printed page, because the humour is in how it's animated. Our stuff is so simple, and depends on timing, which can be hard to explain.'

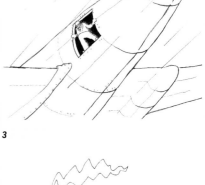

1

2

3

5

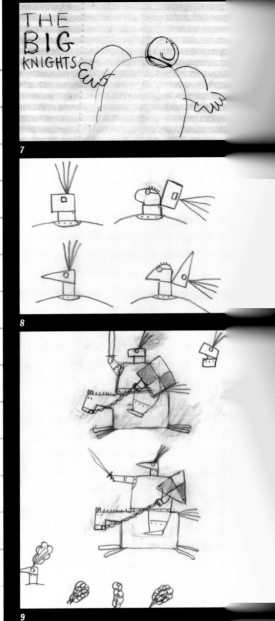

7

8

9

6

(1) Self-portrait by Astley (left) and Baker (right). (2-3) Stills from Neville Astley's earlier films: (2) **Trainspotter** (co-directed with Jeff Newitt) and (3) **The Jump**. (4) A sketch for **The Three Knights**, Baker's undergraduate film.

(5-10) **The Big Knights** series from cut-out to computer: (5-9) Developing character design. As drawing is so labour intensive, they experimented with paper cut-outs articulated with string joints, filming them with an Amiga computer line tester in black and white. Unlike conventional cut-out animation, this technique allowed re-editing (similar to cutting and pasting on a word processor). (5, 10) Another Amiga programme was used for colouring.

Sir Horace the Dog & Sir Doris the Hamster

10

THE BIG KNIGHTS
SIR BORIS & SIR MORRIS

SOUND

NARRATOR: In the far off land of Borovia.

...In the very heart of its untamed interior...

...stands CASTLE BORIS.

...Home of two brothers... Sir Boris and his twin, Sir Morris.

They are the height of TWO men.

...and the weight of FOUR.

ACTION

A large map of the made up country, Borovia.

We track in to a picture of a castle. The sky behind the castle darkens and clouds move across it. There is a flash of lighting.

Another flash of lightning and we cut to Boris and Morris, standing side by side in their underpants. They blink as the narrator talks about them.

A ruler line appears by the side of them, showing that they are about twice the height of an average man.

Some kind of graphic weight scale appears and shows their weight, as they gently rise and fall (as if they were standing on scales).

(1–12) The Big Knights:
(1–6) As the technique was developed (from cut-out to computer) the design became more sophisticated and involved drawing the characters in Adobe Illustrator and importing them into CelAction 2D, the animation program. (7) The final character design; (8) annotated draft script; (9) the fictional geography of the Big Knights' world.

8

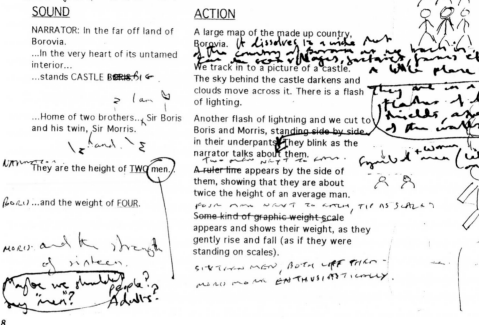

1

2

3

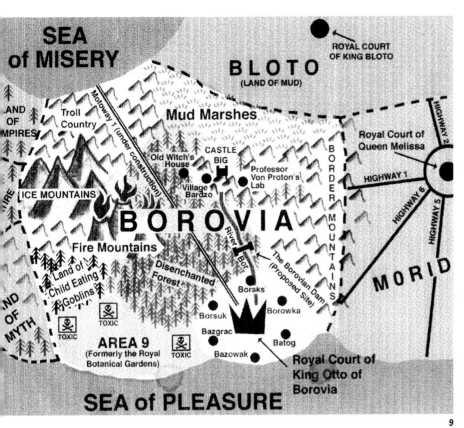

(10–12) Visual 'anachronisms': Coming up with anachronistic spot gags led them to abandon the initial 'Arthurian' setting for the present day – giving greater scope for humour and story. The French medieval village where they wrote some early scripts inspired this change: 'Those shiny new cars in that ancient setting is typical of that mix of old and new world... hence the idea that the locals take dragons and witches for granted as a natural hazard, the way they did the wild boars outside the village.'

9   10

11

12

Previously reluctant to experiment with low-end computers, as the image quality wasn't broadcast quality, they realised that it didn't matter for a trailer. 'The equipment was there, we had no other work on, so why not test it? Our producer Claire Jennings suggested doing a schedule to give a realistic idea of the time it took.' What would have taken six months using conventional animation, took the two of them less than three weeks of animation, and a fortnight colouring. And, 'being straight-ahead animation, it had a human quality to it which computer animation often lacks... In a way, it was exciting again, like being back at college, not knowing exactly how it was going to work out, seeing what you could do.'

The trailer got the BBC involved, and thus began the process of adjusting to TV editorial requirements. 'A ten-minute episode would take too long for everything to be acted purely through sound and visuals, so dialogue is necessary. We hadn't even considered our lack of experience in dialogue writing until it was pointed out – after all, our films, though wordless, did have scripts.' Although the BBC gave them complete freedom on the visual side, writing involved working with other writers and script editors, which initially threw up some problems. 'We came up with a village for one episode, just as a setting (the following

Flashes of thunder and lightning reveal a flapping skull and cross bones flag.

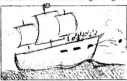

We quickly pull out to reveal a large pirate ship, hurtling through the water, under full sail. Pirates lean out of it, waving cutlasses and shouting. Pull out still further to show that the pirate ship is heading towards another ship.

Standing behind the pirates is their captain, CAPTAIN JOLLY. He has a wooden leg, one hook-hand, an eye-patch and a parrot on his shoulder.) He waves his cutlass, shouting, "ATTACK!"

In long shot, the pirate ship collides with the other ship and the pirates spill out of their own ship, like a swarm of angry wasps.

1

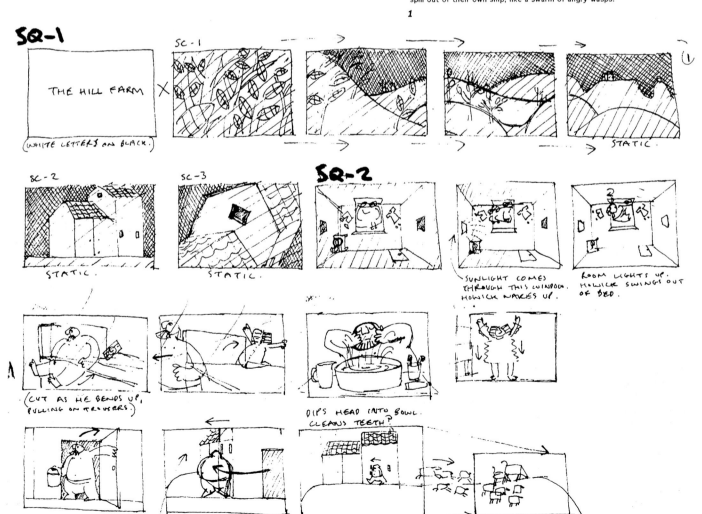

3

week it might be a power station). They came back wanting background on every villager, whereas we'd conceived of them as acting and moving en masse, like "the villagers" in a B movie, with terribly stilted dialogue. It took time to get this through – it's hard when reading someone else's script to know what is intentionally funny or intentionally awkward. And our humour is quite dry – we'd write knowing the delivery would make it funny. Plus the dialogue needed to match the deliberately simple, almost naive, visual style. We wanted this to be a complete world, not a script we just animated.'

Brainstorming produced a list of headings, for example, 'Rust and Knight School' - which generated a two page synopsis; then, with one of the writers (John Sparkes or Gary Parker), they'd 'literally take it to bits'. Sometimes it stayed close to the original, sometimes not. By the end of the day there'd be a structural skeleton and pointers for two episodes. The notes were agreed and then the writer did a first draft, adding details. The BBC would comment and Astley and Baker would do the second draft, bringing it back to something more like an animation script. This pretty much set the structure, although it took another three to four drafts to arrive at the final version.

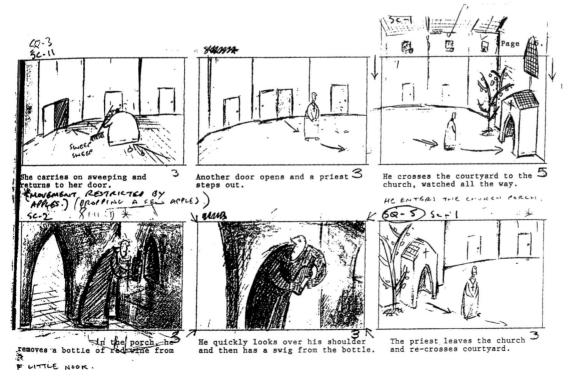

(1–4) Storyboard extracts and character sketches for Baker's earlier shorts: 'With conventional animation, the storyboard is the blueprint, since it is difficult to make changes once animation has been completed.' (1) Early storyboard extract for **Jolly Roger**. (2) Early rough storyboard extract for **The Hill Farm**. (3) Character sketches for the priest in **The Village**. (4) Storyboard extract for **The Village**.

4

```
The Big Knights - Possible episodes:

 1. Anti Knights
 2. Boils and Black Death
 3. Mission Impossible
 4. Time Travel
 5. Knights' Convention
 6. The Dragon
 7. The Evil Wizard/Witch
 8. Vampire - They eat all the garlic and breath vampire
    destroying garlic fumes.
 9. Tidiness
10. A Change of Career
11. No Problem
12. Phantom Castle in Wood
13. A Knight Out
14. Rust
15. Royal Escort
16. Birthday
17. Bewitched
18. Knight School
19. Bad Weather - Such bad weather that they have to
    stay in the castle.
20. Jack and the Beanstalk
21. Paternity Suit
22. Three Wishes
23. Humiliation
24. Holiday
25. Lost Dog
26. Family Reunion
27. Abductees
28. Stress
29. Moving House
30. Lottery
31. Under Siege
32. A Hard Day's Knight
33. Knights in Distress
34. Soothsayer
35. Reading Books
36. Knight Club
37. Knight Mare
```

1

Sir Moris

Thank you, Kind Old Lady! Goodbye!
(To Sir Doris) What a nice little house,
such a sweet old lady...

The old woman transforms herself back into the witch and watches Sir Moris go.
She shakes with frustrated rage. Her whole house is a wreck.

Old Witch

Games! I'll give them Games!

She flies off to the village, on a (broken) broomstick.

Narrator

Meanwhile, back at the village, Sir Boris
has completed all off the games.

Sir Boris bows. Sir Moris walks up behind him.

Sir Moris

Oh no! The Games can't be over already!?

We pan over to the villagers, who are clapping politely and muttering to
themselves. The village is in ruins. Even the children are muted.

Villager One

Well, at least they didn't set fire to the
village this year...

With a flash of lightning, the Old Witch flies into the village.

**The Old Witch (raising her arms above her
head)**

I shall burn your village to the ground!

Flames pour out of her fingertips. Buildings catch fire. Everyone is running
round in circles, screaming.
Sir Moris sees the witch and his face lights up with an enormous grin.

Sir Moris

'Throw the Old Witch! They do have it!

He grabs hold of the witch and hurls her into the air. We pull back to show her

© BBC tv/Mark Baker/Neville Astley 1996 The Big Knights Ltd/Astley Baker Tel/Fax 0171 734 4424   Page 10

2

3

Although initially resistant to working with live-action writers, they learned a lot. 'It's reassuring to find that for everyone who writes, there's no one single moment of inspiration and if it doesn't seem to be working, it doesn't mean everything has to go.' Baker adds, 'The idea there's only one perfect version is simply not true. Sometimes the second drafts didn't seem to work but they became the best ones because quite often, the starting point would turn out to be what was holding us up, and could go.'

'Gradually we realised how good it was to be writing in partnership. Working alone can often be a depressing process – the same thing goes round and round your head and never moves on – so you get a lot just from talking with someone, or even mis-hearing something! When explaining an idea, you start filling in missing bits and acting it out to entertain the other person. We became more relaxed and less precious about allowing other people's input – the way you can be over a short that has become your "art". It's ended up being just as creative, if not more so, than anything else we've done.'

On working with computers, Baker comments, 'when drawing by hand on paper, your pencil is where the line is, whereas with a tablet you're drawing then looking at the screen, and your hand doesn't cover half of the paper. What's good is how quickly you can erase – storyboarding with pencil consumes an enormous amount of rubbers and the paper ends up really dirty – as soon as I've drawn a frame Neville has another idea, so I have to rub it out and draw again, whereas on screen you can delete the line you've drawn and also do multiple deletes to take you back several stages. It's simply a question of habit. One of our animators had programmed his tablet pen so that tapping on the end of it deleted the line. Working on **Jolly Roger**, i.e. pencil on paper, he'd forget and was constantly tapping the end of his pen to make the line disappear!'

The whole team, who knew traditional animation techniques, quickly adapted to the computers. The ease of manipulation meant that Astley and Baker were able to achieve a greater perfection in the final version. 'The computer system meant we had our own editing system – so we could edit as part of the whole process. If we had done the series five years ago on computer, I'd have been trying to make it look like it had been done on paper, something which bothered me when using computers on **Jolly Roger**. Of course we wanted **The Big Knights** to look good, but it doesn't bother me if it looks like it's been done on computer since we've accepted that it's just part of our working method, like the rostrum was.'

(1–4) **The Big Knights:** *(1)* Episode ideas. *(2)* '**The Big Knights** series' tight time schedule meant each storyboard could only be allocated two days. Scripts were laid out in storyboard format, with blank boxes inserted wherever a new shot was needed, and filled in with pencil sketches. Even at this stage, changes could be made to the shot order and some sequences blue-pencilled (i.e. edited out).' *(4)* Sequence of changing storyboards for Village Games episode: 'As **The Big Knights** was created entirely within the computer, the restrictions of storyboard as blueprint didn't apply. All elements, including design, animation and layout, could be adjusted at any stage of the production process.'

4

SIR BORIS
Was that you?

24/8

SIR MORRIS
I don't think so.

24/9

THE SMOKE

As/ clears, they see the old witch as she really is for the first time.

24/10

HOPPING UP AND DOWN.

SIR MORRIS
(overwhelmed)
Boris! Look! A real old witch!

C/U on Sir Morris, his eyes filled with tears. He's like a man reunited with a long lost love. Beautiful, romantic music. Soft focus vignette.

SIR BORIS
(oov, interrupting his reverie)
Me first!

24/11

SLOW MOTION 24/12

Cut to Sir Boris, who grabs the old witch

BORIS EXITS FRAME

HE THROWS HER.

24/13B

and she soars out of frame.

WITCH
Aaaarrrgghh!

24/14B

24/13A

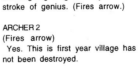

24/14A

24/14C

24/15

SIR MORRIS
I wanted to **throw her** first.

FOLLOWING WITCH WITH EYES

24/16

SIR BORIS
You can have the **next turn**. Come on! Let's see where she **landed.**

24/17

(BORIS WALKS IN FRONT OF MORRIS)

25/1

WIPE TO THE VILLAGE GAMES.

A couple of archers fire their bows.

25/2

ARCHER 1
Sending Big Knights away was stroke of genius. (Fires arrow.)

ARCHER 2
(Fires arrow)
Yes. This is first year village has not been destroyed.

25/3

(BOTH ARROWS HIT BULL'S EYE.)

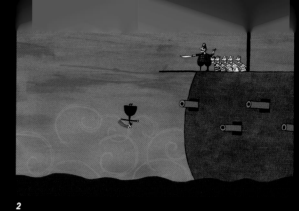

1

2

5

6

7

8

9

(1–9) Colour design: (1–4) Stills from **Jolly Roger**; (5–9) Stills from **The Big Knights**. As the memory required for the kind of background textures used in **Jolly Roger** would have slowed down the computer, a design decision was made to work exclusively with flat colour on **The Big Knights**. Many layers of overlays, shadows and areas of slight colour shifts were used to give depth to the image. Each episode had its own colour palette, largely dictated by the story's setting.

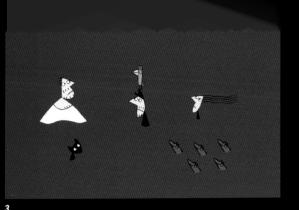

3

4

camera 1 (opening shot)

camera 2

camera 3

camera 4

camera 5

10

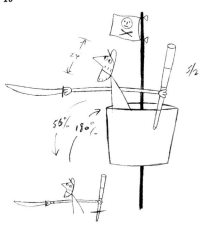

11

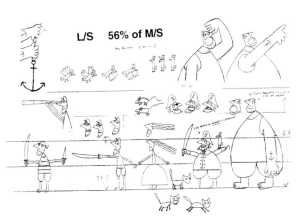

L/S   56% of M/S

(1–11) Traditional and computer techniques compared: 'Jolly Roger' was traditionally animated, i.e. drawn frame-by-frame on sheets of paper, then scanned into the Animo computer and coloured digitally. Drawings were produced at one of three sizes, depending on whether the action was in long-shot, medium-shot or close-up. Guides at these three scales (L/S, M/S and C/S) were produced, to help the animators draw the characters in correct proportion. *(11)* Thumbnail sketches from **Jolly Roger**, used to work out action and poses. Interestingly, even in **The Big Knights'** computer production, similar thumbnails were often drawn by hand as guides for the animation. However, **The Big Knights** used no paper drawings for artwork – which was made to one absolute scale, within the computer. This meant that a shot originally animated in close-up could easily be re-framed as a long-shot, or vice versa. *(10)* The backgrounds were like virtual sets. A scene would be set up complete with characters and props in full colour; then camera positions assigned to match the storyboard frames. Animation would then begin. In this respect, the technique has similarities with a model shoot, rather than traditional "flat" animation.' Further information on techniques can be found at: www.astleybaker.co.uk

John Cary

Series production

As a children's animation producer, John Cary begins developing a project in one of three ways. He will either find an existing property, write an original idea, or work with a writer on an original concept. 'What's important every time is finding the magic nugget inside that makes the property work, for example, talking trains, a cowardly pirate, a boy with magic boots or a friendly spider. Once identified, it needs to be tested in different situations, amplified, and have each subsidiary idea tested against the central one.'

Before writing Cary works with others to create character descriptions, settings and rough plot outlines, what he describes as 'a Bible that everyone works to'. They will define character relationships and talk about visual interpretation. 'Collaboration is built into the whole process from the start. First you hire a writer, then a designer, other artists, actors, an animation director and an editor; although "collaboration" smacks too much of democracy – you need colleagues who will take your vision and, hopefully, improve on it. Part of my role is mediating between all the creative parties.'

Cary was drawn to **Captain Pugwash** – famously remembered as a cut-out puppet animation TV series from the late '50s – by John Ryan's original books' cinematic-quality iillustrations and classic sitcom set-up. The characters in **Captain Pugwash** live at close quarters, and with the ever-present threat of the pirate protagonists, there is plenty of potential for adventure. 'In commercial terms, pirates are universal. Pugwash is funny, as are the other characters, and both the books and the series were well-known and loved. But

there were commercial considerations to work out with our financiers, the Britt Allcroft company. Pugwash was perceived as old-fashioned and very British – hence the need for a new international setting and some additional characters.'

As **Captain Pugwash** was an existing property with its own visual language, the challenge was to retain its original flavour while adapting it for the present day. The background style was changed but the original characters stayed faithful to the old ones. 'The characters are an animator's nightmare since they all have spotty shirts, stripy headbands and stripy sashes. Pugwash has a vast lace collar, but over-simplifying it would make him unrecognisable from the old days. We covered that by referring back to the old cut-out style, which saves re-drawing the bodies – particularly the details – and gives the overall animation a cut-out feel. The director's job is to know both when to stick to that style and make it simpler for the animators, and also when to come out of it for a particular gesture which has to be animated traditionally.'

Cary sees his role of producer as putting art and money together as an integrated mind set. 'The priority in series animation is to maintain creativity in a context of volume production over a short period of time. The director, Colin White and I have quite distinct roles. I come in at the story outline, script and drafts stage. I supervise the recording, along with the dialogue director. I'll look at the storyboards because I like to see what's going through, and then look at the animatic – but once it gets into the actual animation direction and supervising the art direction, the director takes over.'

1

© John Ryan 2000

2

3

© John Ryan 2

5

6

7

(1-7) Updating the cast for **Captain Pugwash**: The original series' Barnabas is replaced by Caribbean Jonah and a new female character, Maggie Lafayette, is also added. *(1)* The updated Captain Pugwash, Caribbean Jonah, Maggie Lafayette, and *(7)* Barnabas. *(2-3)* Original illustrations by the creator of **Captain Pugwash**, writer and illustrator John Ryan showing the cabin boy Tom representing the audience. *(4)* Ryan's wife, Priscilla, moving cardboard 'puppets' in real time in front of a film camera for the original series. The first **Captain Pugwash** episode was transmitted on the 8th October 1957. The first few episodes were transmitted live. *(5-6)* Puppets with levers showing.

2

1 **3**

(1–9) Reinterpretation of **Captain Pugwash:** *(1–2)* John Ryan's painting style and his British-looking backgrounds. These were transformed into the Spanish Main. *(4)* The '30s poster used as a model for the new background style. *(5)* Ryan's original pirate ship, the 'Black Pig', moved along a curtain rail. *(6)* The first computer model of the 'Black Pig'; (7) working model; *(8–9)* the wire frame guide and the final rendering.

4

5

8

6   7   9

'When the rushes come back from the overseas studio, I then put on my editor's hat and watch the overall film with the director. He supervises all the minor changes and I get heavily involved with the sound effects and laying the music before the final cut – a very traditional producer's role in the old-fashioned feature film tradition (script, casting and music). I also do a bit more on the scripting and recording. If we disagree on how to express certain things within the film, I am happy to leave it to my director.'

The focus is on maximum creative value on screen. 'You put values on certain production areas, looking for where you can get the biggest bang for your buck – such as the script, storyboarding, maximising the re-use of backgrounds, planning for effective use of animation, sound effects and off-screen voices.' Using 3D shots costs four or five times more than using ordinary shots, but according to Cary, 'even if it's just for five per cent of the show, 30 seconds in ten minutes, it's so impressive – it will carry through with the audience, who'll come away feeling they've seen a very high-quality show.'

Cary's background is in live-action and film editing, so he approaches animation in the same way he would film. 'A lot of animated series in the West are created in this rather old-fashioned, almost theatrical way. Traditionally, animators clear the stage, bring their characters on, do an act, depart, and so on to the next act. I see shots as viewpoints on a 3D world.'

'I admire Japanese animation for its tremendous sense of frame composition, its real use of the camera, its perspective and deep perspective. In our productions we put objects known as "dingles" in the foreground, normally painted very dark so you have a sense of the camera intruding on the action. Interestingly, John Ryan's original **Pugwash** had dingles, but they were there to cover up the workings of the levers driving the characters. So, what for John Ryan was a practical solution to a problem, becomes for us a whole approach to composition and art direction. The point is, backgrounds shouldn't simply be paintings behind the action, but represent different camera viewpoints.'

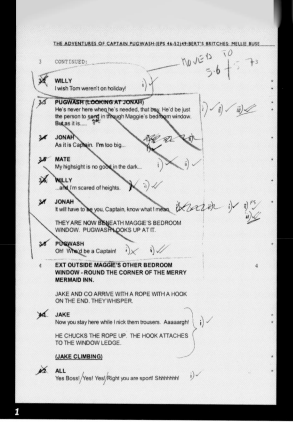

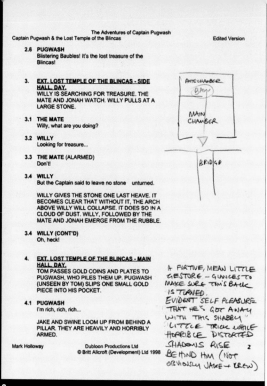

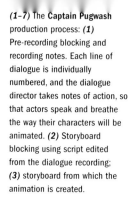

2

Mark Holloway

(1–7) The **Captain Pugwash** production process: *(1)* Pre-recording blocking and recording notes. Each line of dialogue is individually numbered, and the dialogue director takes notes of action, so that actors speak and breathe the way their characters will be animated. *(2)* Storyboard blocking using script edited from the dialogue recording; *(3)* storyboard from which the animation is created.

The Adventures of Captain Pugwash

STORYBOARD For The Episode

THE TEMPLE OF THE BLINCAS

By KEITH SCOBLE
For
Dubloon Productions Limited
JANUARY 1999

1/1

NARR: THE ANCIENT TEMPLE OF THE BLINCA PEOPLE WAS SET HIGH ON THE PEAK OF MONTE PLENO...

1/2

...CAPTAIN PUGWASH'S GUIDE BOOK SAID THAT

1/3

NAR. "THERE WAS TREASURE BURIED IN THE RUINS"

1/4

TOM EXAMINES THE ALTER - PUGWASH READING FROM A GUIDE BOOK PUGWASH " THE ANCIENT BLINCA PEOPLE KEPT..."

1/5

TOM PUZZLED. PUSHES ALTER. IT MOVES A LITTLE.

PUG .V.O. "HUGE QUANTITIES OF GOLD IN THEIR.."

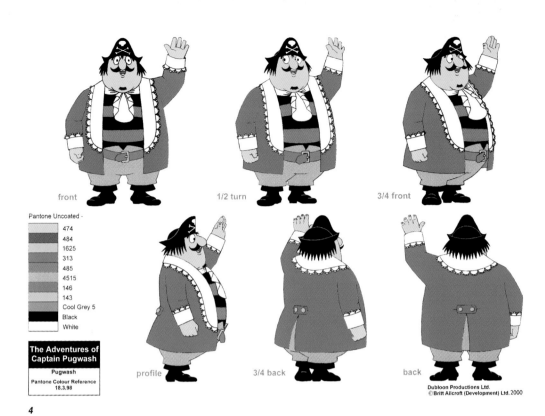

front   1/2 turn   3/4 front

Pantone Uncoated -

474
484
1625
313
485
4515
146
143
Cool Grey 5
Black
White

The Adventures of Captain Pugwash

Pugwash

Pantone Colour Reference
18.3.98

profile   3/4 back   back

Dubloon Productions Ltd.
©Britt Allcroft (Development) Ltd. 2000

(4) Character model sheet for **Captain Pugwash**. *(5)* Bar sheets for two seconds of film. The voice track is analysed phonetically frame-by-frame so that animators can move mouths in synch. *(6)* Action timing: the director's frame-by-frame instructions to the animators. *(7)* **Line test**; *(8)* Director's notes on line test.

7

4

5

The Adventures of Captain Pugwash   episode name 32 Temple of Blincas   scene number   sheet number   John Cary Studios. 1999

DIAL. 1 | B | B | B | B | AH | | SIL | K | AH | T | TH | R | OW | | T | | JH | EY |
337   353   369

DIAL. 2   B - b-b - b -but   It's Cut-throat   Jake

ACTION

CAM.

6

The Adventures of Captain Pugwash   episode name 32 Temple of Blincas   scene number   sheet number 4   Dubloon Productions Ltd. 1998

© Britt Allcroft (Development) Ltd. 2000

8

PRODUCCION
CAPTAIN PUGW.   CAM 2

EPISODIO	ESTUDIO	FECHA	TAPE
032	CARTOON P	16-6-99	03

ADD A BLINK TO JONATHAN AT END

Sq./Sc.	Ftg.	
2/5	100	DUST DON'T WORK IT HAVE INCREASE DON'T DO CIRCLE GOING TO ONE SIDE. YES ALSO CHECK SYNC - WILLY SAYS PUGWASH'S LINE 'IMRICH' - OR APPEARS TO - MAYBE THE TRACK IS OUT AND IT'S HIS 'OO ECK'
3/1	138	CHECK PUGWASH SHOULDERS AND TOM OUT OF MODEL WHEN HE TURN. YES. SHOULDERS DEFINITELY NOT ON MODEL. LINETEST MISTAKE ON PUGLASHS EYES.
3/2	73	JAKES ARM SHAKING IS TOO EVENLY TIMED - IT SHOULD ACCENT THE DIALOGUE (IT ISN'T SLUGGED) - BIGGER MOVEMENTS FOR MORE EMPHASIS.
3/3	80	HOOK UP JAKES ACTION SO HIS HEAD CONTINUES THE MOVE UP TO ACCENT "HANDS".
3/4	64	LIP SYNCH IS OFF - (SLIPPED TRACK?) BIGGER HAND MOVE TO EMPHASISE 'STOP ME
5/1	111	JAKE IS GREAT LOSE THIS TOM POSE (AFTER HE'S PUT PLATE DOWN - HE LOOKS LIKE A RABBIT. KEEP HIS HANDS ON THE PLATE FOR THE HOLD THEN INBETWEEN HIM BACK INTO THE HOLE.
5/2	51	JAKE HAVE POINTING DOWN, FOLLOWING ACTION OF 5/1 WHEN TURN HAND HE HAS MOVE HIS ARM TO. YES - START HIS ARM UP AS ENDS 5/1 - BRING IT DOWN AT BEGINNING TO SCENE FOR "OR YOU'LL" INTO YOUR PRESENT START POSE
5/3	24	OK
5/4	26	START EXPRESSION JAKE AS IN STORY NO! THIS SCENE IS OK I ASKED FOR THE GRIN IN THE SLUGGING
5/5	21	LAST POSE AS 5/8 IT IS! THIS SCENE IS OK.

For **Captain Pugwash**, Cary had the town and harbour where the pirates live, and the ships, designed in much the same way as he would with a live-action set. There is a real sense of being able to navigate through the world of Pugwash. As well as adding conviction, this makes for more interesting camera angles and easier storyboarding, since the artist simply has to look at the overall production design and 'place' themselves in the 'set' to make it work.

'A lot of series dialogue editing suffers from the "I'll say a line – you say a line" approach. I prefer lively and realistic dialogue that informs recording – usually line-by-line to allow for overlapping dialogue where necessary.' Series animation is often done mid- or close mid-shot, which can give a rather uninteresting texture to the camera work and filmmaking. Cary prefers more contrast between long-shots and close-ups. 'I've told everyone at the studio, this is a dissolve-free zone. Time and location change can be easily done with cutting, and audiences will follow it. In animation filmmaking you have to create all the elements separately without the benefit of seeing sound and picture together until the very end. The skill is to imagine and predict the missing pieces.'

In the process of creating **Captain Pugwash** Cary and his team had a chance to explore the advantages that computers can offer. 'Sailing ships are technically difficult for the animators, so we decided to look into how we could build them on computer. We were using authentic 16th-century naval designs, so the drawings could be printed out and then traced by the animator. But then our 3D modeller pushed things a lot further and found we could generate an entire scene in 3D. We had close-ups of decks and interiors and medium-shots of the ships at sea. Where they don't have to be animated as a 3D shot within a 3D environment we can choose an appropriate angle for that shot, print the angle of the ship out in colour – or create a colour file – then deliver it to the studio to be composited into the backgrounds. Moving seas can be included in the 2D rather like a back projection plate in live-action.' However, Cary concludes that computers are best used to achieve things otherwise too expensive or laborious. 'They're most useful behind the scenes: storyboarding on Photoshop, non-linear editing, spreadsheets for budgets and databases for archive retrieval.'

(1–5) The second half of the **Captain Pugwash** production process: *(1)* Recording in the master music library. The programme is now ready for the addition of sound effects and music. *(2)* The score for 'Ahoy, Me Hearties!' *(3–4)* Each drawing is scanned into the computer and painted digitally, using the Animo system. Each scene consists of up to 20 levels or layers, which are arranged and combined: the Animo compositing system replaces the old rostrum camera in this respect. *(5)* Final episode shot using Cary Studio's 3D system.

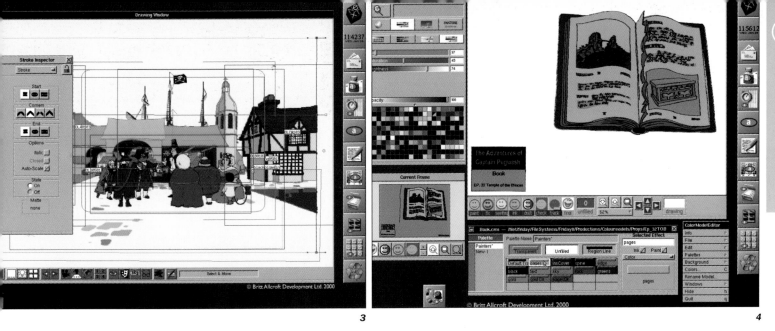

3

4

5

Simon Pummell

Advanced production techniques

Pummell's work challenges all conventional definitions of animation through its complex, technically innovative production techniques. His work has broken new ground in its use of shadow animation, layering, digital manipulation and compositing. The films often employ mixtures of advanced and basic technologies in unexpected ways. Though highly diverse in subject matter and look, the films all deal with anxieties around the human body, technology and one's place in the self and in the world.

'Often a project first announces itself as a cluster of images, which, despite no obvious context, persist, as if looking for a home in some sort of narrative. I hang on to these floating images, and return and play with them until they gradually reveal themselves. Sometimes images seem to form a particular project, but then if that dies, they might migrate to another project.'

Pummell finds that there is usually an intensive random research period of looking for information, images or text to use. 'If something snags my interest or if it creates a certain anxiety then that material will be collected, even when it does not fit a more conscious structuring of the piece.' For Pummell, this has increasingly become the fashioning of narrative, although more abstract films or projects similar to a hypertext installation are conceived in the same way.

'Sometimes it's quite an intellectual process - almost juggling with ideas and formal approaches - sometimes it's quite down to earth, just collecting and experimenting with objects and tools. I've realised the quality of the final film and the passion of the research are directly linked. Still, nothing ever works out as expected, which is why there is no substitute for the practice of actually making things.'

1

2

(1–5) Stills from **The Secret Joy of Falling Angels**: 'The film depicts a confrontation, full of ambiguous attraction and fear, between a woman and a winged figure, inspired by 15th-century depictions of the Annunciation. The angel is simultaneously super- and sub-human.'

'Both Disney and the great Renaissance artists built up figures in the same way: out of simple ovoids. Michelangelo would use two hundred to build the muscles on a back; Disney would use seven to create a whole character. The film's character animation was an attempt to fall somewhere in the middle – using the principle of squash and stretch with relatively complex bodies.'

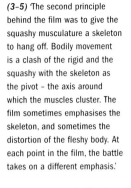

 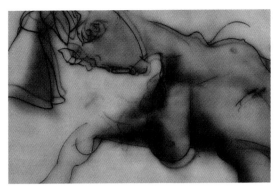

(3-5) 'The second principle behind the film was to give the squashy musculature a skeleton to hang off. Bodily movement is a clash of the rigid and the squashy with the skeleton as the pivot – the axis around which the muscles cluster. The film sometimes emphasises the skeleton, and sometimes the distortion of the fleshy body. At each point in the film, the battle takes on a different emphasis.'

 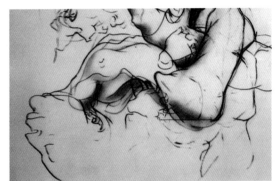

'Annabelle's music for **The Secret Joy of Falling Angels,** and its use of the human voice came from her training as an opera singer. In the film the woman's voice singing on the soundtrack functions as the woman Mary's voice. It is ethereal and distant when she's inside the cage, whereas when she's transforming into more cartoony shapes, scat singing has been recorded and sung closely into the microphone, with a breathy, jazzy sound. Finally, when the Angel and Mary have sex at the end of the film, the ethereal vocal is recorded in a similar way and as such, the two styles merge.'

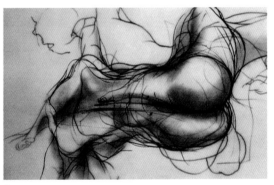 

3

4   5

'TV tends to commission for particular time slots, which determine financial and time constraints. That's fine. The pressure helps squeeze the material into its final shape: compromise being the condition of any work existing in the world.' For Pummell, writing and storyboarding are simply different methods of visualising and annotating. 'Sometimes I'll sit and draw out a scene, then re-write it as text back into the script. Writing and drawing can kick off different associations in the brain. The script is a detailed representation of how I visualise the work, and both can change as the project grows. The ratio of change to persistence is often the key to the work. The more you plan, the more committed your vision is early in the process; paradoxically, you then have more freedom to change. If there is no evolution, your first draft becomes your final work. Revision and evolution is the real work for me.'

'Every stage of the production process has different pains and pleasures. Shooting is probably the most exciting and scary – the drop is also the furthest and the wire the highest during shooting. I expect the relationship with a producer to be very collaborative and to affect every area of the film. Film is a material and technological medium, hence financing, organising, visualising and executing are all interdependent. I work closely with my producer and my business partner Janine Marmot on every stage of a project – from concept to post-production.

'Working with my first producer, Keith Griffiths, on **The Secret Joy of Falling Angels** was a pragmatic learning curve – or a reality check! I had this over-ambitious live-action feature film project of a tragic story about a transexual, intercut with animated sequences of the 12 stations of the cross. Keith suggested I make the Annunciation segment as a short for British TV's Channel 4. This became **The Secret Joy of Falling Angels**. Having forced me to be realistic he then rigorously defended my right to make the film as I wanted to.'

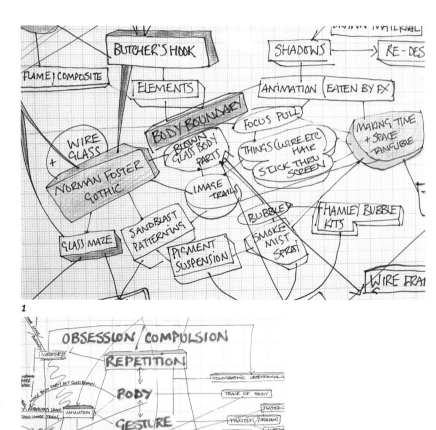

1

2

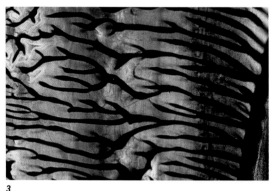

3

4

5

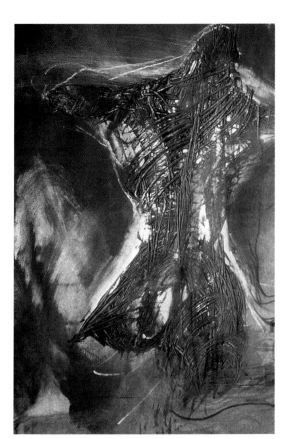

6

(1–7) Butcher's Hook: The techniques used throughout the film range from shadow puppets, through charcoal and graphite drawings, to abstract screens of feathery texture created using the surface tension of oil and acrylic paint. 'I wanted the film to be a mini encyclopaedia of animation techniques', says Pummell. **(1–2)** Conceptual diagrams; **(6–7)** early developmental paintings. **(8)** Development painting for **Rose Red** in watercolour of a struggling figure. **(9) Rose Red**, a science fiction thriller that further explores this motif of the trapped body, central in **The Secret Joy of Falling Angels** and **Butcher's Hook**.

7

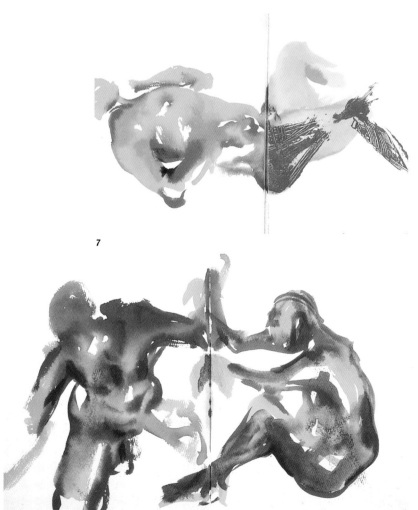

8

9

BUTCHERS HOOK

Barrie Houghton

(1–4) **Butcher's Hook**. The narrative follows a taxidermist, who is attacked and transformed by his menagerie of perfectly preserved dead animals, ending up as a specimen himself. 'The film is composed of photographic images, rather than drawn: from a belief that the human face in close-up is the most compelling image in cinema. We will follow a face into the most extraordinary worlds: here, one of shadows and dead animals. Yet the film also contains an enormous amount of "drawing". Working with film-quality compositing post-production tools, the film re-draws and re-forms the images, layer upon layer, radically re-adjusting the balance of photo and graphic.'

'The compositing and digital manipulation was done by Ant Walsham, who was heavily involved in fundamental decisions such as the degree and quality of translucence in the images. Integrating the taxidermist into the world of shadows and glass was the result of a three-way interaction between Ant, myself and what the technology could do at the time.'

'Editing combinations of live-action and animation has particular problems. **Butcher's Hook** was storyboarded in collaboration with The Mill post-production studios. The animation was then all shot, and effectively edited in camera, given the labour-intensive nature of animation. At that point the first cut was made, and the live-action was shot to fit into that first cut. With any film like this you are editing on two axes at once: the usual horizontal lines of time and narrative, and also building up layers of images laid over each other into any single shot.' (3–4) Creating the shadow animation for **Butcher's Hook**.

2

3

4

Simon Pummell's film **The Temptation of Sainthood** had ambitious special effects and was completed at top London post-production house, The Mill, with people whom Pummell had worked with before on commercials. For Pummell, their collaborative work created the visual language of the film. 'It was another example of producing a choice which was in fact a creative one. Such relationships are key because they give you access to a huge creative team of technicians and technical possibilities. Pat Joseph at The Mill can break a project down and take you through the storyboard in a way that clarifies and makes achievable the images you are trying to create. For me, collaboration is about making space for people to contribute, with their own creative obsessions. I feel it's really cooking when people produce things you'd never have thought of.'

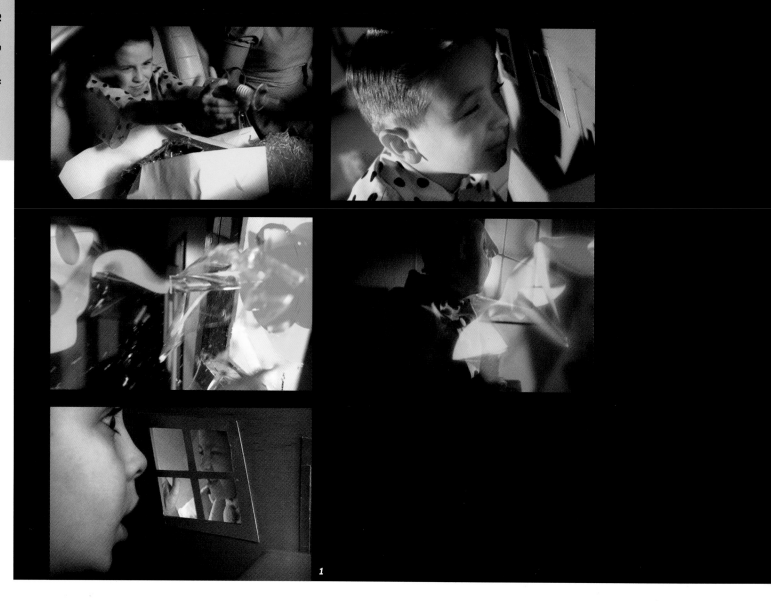

1

'My films don't have sound so closely synchronised to the image, it always comes after the fine cut... I've mainly worked with two sound people: Larry Sider and Annabelle Pangborn. Particularly with more fantastical animation, Larry believes that sound is your live-action track. Because sound is so specific, it creates the space in which the film is taking place. Whether it is huge or tiny, arid or watery has enormous impact on the audience, even if they are not consciously aware of it. Larry builds very dense sound composites. The wings in **The Secret Joy of Falling Angels** were combinations of many sounds, ranging from pigeon wing flaps to the rustling of shaken silk scarves. Sound is 50 per cent of the film, as it brings scale and scope to a short.'

'I don't live a compartmentalised life. You can never tell what might or might not feed into your work. In the end, you're only likely to grow as a filmmaker if you develop as a person. And who knows what might cause that. My training was first in literary critical analysis, which is basically just how to take texts apart. I find the labyrinthine quality of modernist literature with its layers of accumulated meanings very seductive. I then trained as a filmmaker, not an animator; so for me animation is a technique I use rather than a defining calling.'

Pummell is now involved in writing features, and is much more interested in conventional narrative, partly because he finds a feature's time span is long enough for a narrative to accumulate real weight. 'In shorts I've always been interested in cramming big and allusive narratives into a short time frame. Personally, short films are more satisfying as puzzles than as little stories. I believe as filmmakers we can learn from a thousand years of storytelling in literature and painting. It seems arrogant to imagine that film somehow made all that accumulated knowledge obsolete. As new media grows, film is beginning to take its place in the history of media, and needs to expand and absorb new influences. It seems that film at the moment needs to look backwards and forwards. Just as, when they started, the movies influenced the narrative techniques of the novel and painting; now it seems likely that the explosion of non-linear digital media will change how films look and tell stories.'

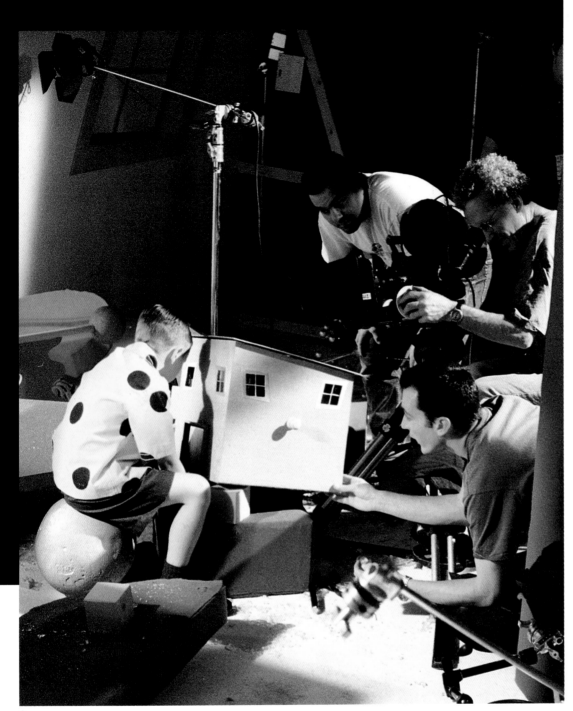

(1–3) **Ray Gun Fun** is a cartoon created in 3D, about a little boy left alone with a ray gun and a doll's house, whose fantasies prove more dangerous than expected.

'The control of the colour, the shapes and the movements came through post-production techniques which allow each frame – and each layer of each frame – to be manipulated like a cel in a cartoon. Whether the action was shot as live-action or model (and it was often shot as both), there is no pixelation. Each movement was shot at different speeds, then treated like a sheaf of drawings. In digital post-production each layer of each frame was riffled through, then shuffled and re-adjusted to create new movements and tempos.'

(1) Stills; *(2)* production still of the boy and doll's house; *(3)* photographer John McMurtrie set up the 'time-slice' shoot which involves a ring of cameras on tripods. This time-slice technique allows for each frame, once photographed, to be scanned into the computer and digitally morphed into the next, resulting in a slow, smooth rotating image.

2

3

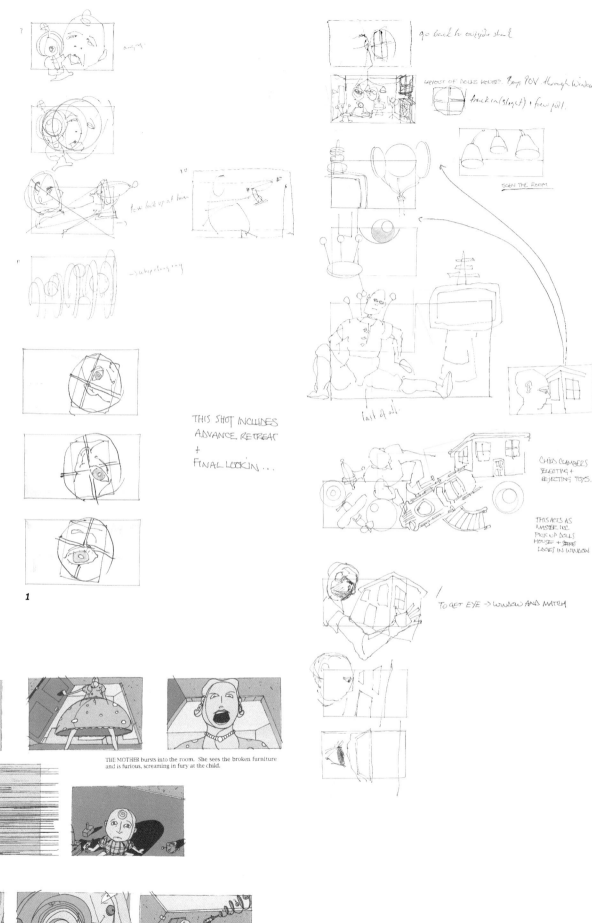

go back to outside shot

LAYOUT OF DOLLS HOUSE: Boy's POV through Window
track in (slog L) + focus pull.

SCAN THE ROOM

THIS SHOT INCLUDES
ADVANCE RETREAT
+
FINAL LOOKIN ...

1

last of all

CHILD CLAMBERS
SELECTING +
REJECTING TOYS.

THIS ACTS AS
MASTER INC
PICK UP DOLLS
HOUSE + SHED
LOOKS IN WINDOW

TO GET EYE → WINDOW AND MATCH

HIS 3 "SELVES" EXCHANGE LOOKS...

THE MOTHER bursts into the room. She sees the broken furniture
and is furious, screaming in fury at the child.

2

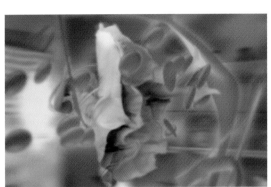

3

(1–3) **Ray Gun Fun:** *(1)* Pummell's rough shooting storyboard drawn in pen and ink; *(2)* a later production storyboard drawn in the style of a comic strip by Julian Henshaw, transcribed from Pummell's earlier rough storyboards. *(3)* A sequence from the finished film, using the time-slice technique.

'In that way new digital media are following a tradition,' Pummell continues. 'The avant-garde of any given medium often creates the popular forms of the subsequent medium. For example, painting struggled for multiple viewpoints in cubism just as film montage was being established. In the same way, breaking up the filmic picture plane (for instance, using frames within frames) has tended to be avant-garde in film, but popular in TV, and now it is becoming a regular feature in games. This is a central issue in **Dogfight**, the feature film I'm currently developing. It's an adaptation of William Gibson's short story by the same name, and is structured around the playing of a game – a classic narrative device. However, the game is a holographic flight simulation game and the protagonist learns to play using real historical archive footage. In this way the game becomes part of telling the story, acting as a prism for the conflict in the narrative and adding context and depth. By presenting all this within the game, it becomes acceptable for the film frame to be fractured and written across.'

Gil Alkabetz

Focusing on form

Some filmmakers have an animation style that is instantly recognisable in every film, but for Gil Alkabetz, every new project is a challenge to do something quite visually different. This can be a very demanding process. 'If you have a particular style', Alkabetz explains, 'you create a particular world whose rules you know, so you can play with breaking them. Hence the style can dictate the kind of stories you invent, and the cinematic language you use. By not being committed to any one style, you somehow have to reinvent the wheel every time. I know I can't say anything new, so my point is to say it in a new way. Making a film is to define animation anew every time.'

His design and formal concerns are reflected in the directors he admires, such as Paul Driessen, Phil Mulloy, Igor Kovalyov, Mark Baker and Michaela Pavlatova. 'They are virtuoso storytellers – one of the most difficult things in animation – and their work is beautifully designed.'

Maybe because of his training as a graphic designer, Alkabetz needs to find something that works visually in formal terms in order to proceed further with a film idea. Unless he can abstract and simplify his graphic forms, he abandons the project; which inevitably means a great deal of work is thrown away.

Swamp, a film about the stupidity of war, features two heavily armoured cavalry battalions fighting for giant balloons to save them from sinking into the swamp. His decision to have no visual reference to the swamp at all was the point at which he knew it would work as an animation film, since every film idea has to answer his self-imposed question: 'Why should it be in animation?' In making the swamp invisible, Alkabetz explores the film frame itself: 'We know the swamp exists because of what happens, and from the sound, so there's a play between what happens in the film and what happens out of frame'.

'**An idea appeals** when it has a certain degree of abstraction: that's why my themes are quite general. Unlike live-action, where characters have to be individualised, in animation they can be more generalised and representative.' Alkabetz does not see himself as a natural storyteller and envies those with a gift for plot inventiveness. 'Working out a kind of mathematical formula, such as the laws of gravity in **Swamp**, helps me find a solid basis on which to build the plot, such as it is, and determine how things will develop. The characters are unable to influence the events – they are subordinated to the given situation. The more passive they are, the better the plot.' The tension between the set-up and its logical development to absurd extremes provides the humour in both **Swamp** and **Rubicon**.

1

Yankale originated in a short story he'd read about a man in his 30s still living with his oppressive mother, and reluctantly coming to terms with the requirements of adulthood. To become an integrated member of society and a useful citizen, he must relinquish his childish side. 'This is considered a necessary and positive process', Alkabetz comments, 'but I think it also has negative aspects, such as the loss of childhood fantasy and imagination, and becoming just like everyone else.' It was not until he started drawing plus and minus signs, and combining them as crosses, that he found the design for the film and thought 'finally that maybe there was a reason to make it'.

2

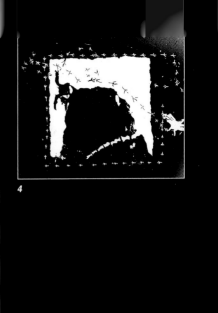

4

(1) Self-portrait. *(2–4)* **Bitzbutz**: Plasticine on glass. A black monster and a white bird emerge from a white square and fight for territorial possession, finally erasing one another. Alkabetz enjoyed the material's physical resistance and the potential for improvisation, as when the plasticine broke, it left bits which added texture, like ink splodges.

(5–7) **Swamp**: Made at the Film Akademie in Stuttgart. The watercolour used for the balloons reinforces the visual paradox, i.e. that they are lifting impossibly heavy weights.

5

6

7

1

2

3

4

5

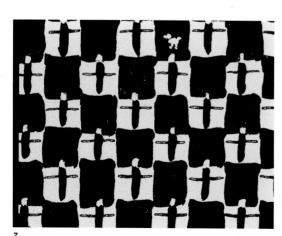

6

7

8

(1–13) **Yankale:** *(1–8)* The plus and minus signs and cross motifs that crystallised the film's design. *(9–13)* The bright pink and soft rounded contours of the sequence in which Yankale recalls his childhood as a joyful desert island fantasy. This contrasts with the sharp black lines of adult life and the routine of work, which appear angled and restrictive.

9

10

11

12

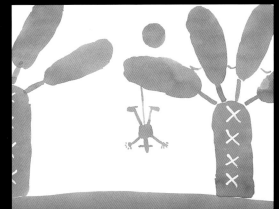

13

7

The rower looks like a sheep, the sheep looks like the rower

The head switched with the cabbage

The rower rows with the wolf

The sound of the water disappeared, the rower has cotton-wool in his ears

1

2

A → B

3

4

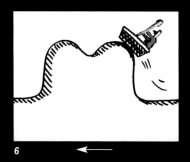

A Riddle:
A Wolf, a sheep and a cabbage need to cross the river.
How can you bring them across, one by one, without the sheep eating the cabbage, nor the wolf eating the sheep?

5

6

(1–12) Rubicon: (1–4) The film began with a sketch of three figures. Playing with the forms was the only way Alkabetz could find the story: 'Should there be relationships between them? Should the wolf be in love with the sheep? Is the cabbage maybe their baby?' **(5)** He also wanted a political subtext, and thought of the riddle which could also apply to the Middle Eastern situation: 'One moment it looks like there can be a solution, the next it doesn't work; and nobody understands why. The bad guys and the good guys seem interchangeable, or they keep changing roles, they shake hands then they go to war again...'

(6) Extract from an early **Rubicon** storyboard which features the water line as a protagonist. To save time he omitted this when line-testing, then realised it looked better without. It also would have required an extra cel layer and affected other elements to be animated. In the initial print, the river crossings were too fast to read, so he put in two seconds of white throughout which took it from five minutes in length to seven minutes, and he found that then it worked. In the final scenes the characters exchange voices: the sheep howls like a wolf; the cabbage bleats like a sheep; and the wolf doesn't make a sound. It's good to end on a high point – a pre-end credit punchline. **(7–10)** Initially he storyboarded flags on the boat, to underscore the political subtext, but later cut them, since they had already served their purpose as a kind of building block. **(11–12)** Stills from the final film.

8

The rower takes the sheep out of his ears, the sound of the water comes back

The cabbage disappeared, the rower picks his nose

And blows the cabbage out of it

9

The rudder disappeared

The wolf shows the rower where it is

The sheep flies in the air ahead of the boat

The boat sails ahead of the cabbage

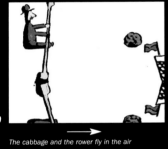

10

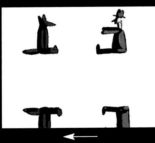

The cabbage and the rower fly in the air

The boat and the rudder disappeared

The rower and the sheep float upon the river (no boat)

The rower and the cabbage float, half sunk, in the river

11

12

1

2

Elements are scanned into the computer as cut-outs, then animated.

(4–6) Commissioned work, from Nickelodeon stings to rock promos. 'In one sense this is easier, since it is working to a defined brief, but then the client can change things. I try and be a good servant. Sometimes it takes you in unexpected directions, you come across something new or find a solution you can use in your own work.'

(Next page, 1–3) Illustrations: As there is no funding for short, personal animation films in Israel, Alkabetz worked as an illustrator for several years, until he was offered the opportunity to work in Germany. *(3)* Cover illustration for Belgian animation magazine Plateau.

Most of Alkabetz' subsequent ideas for a film come when storyboarding, although deciding when to actually start this process can be critical. 'If I start too early, I will destroy it. I need a structure before I start, but it cannot be too rigid, as this can impede the flow of visual development.' He draws an enormous number of storyboards, seeking the right balance between story and formal elements, and keeps going until it feels right. 'If I try to mentally visualise the narrative, it just doesn't work, I have to see it on paper. I have to know where it's going. If I don't, I'm in trouble.'

Although some people see animation as simply the laborious part of a creative process, for Alkabetz it's the basic art – 'there's no limit to what you can invent. I don't rehearse when I'm animating in the sense of acting things out. I work straight ahead. For the animation to feel natural, I have to work fast in quite a sketchy manner, as long as it looks fluent I can add detail later.'

3

Taurus

Gemini

Virgo

Cancer

Leo

4

Preferring to do most of the work himself, Alkabetz feels that making a film should not take longer than 18 months to maintain the energy level and the style. He tends to reject ideas which would involve a lot of people. 'I'm very bad at brainstorming. I can't think with groups of people, I need to consult only after I have the basic concept, then sometimes people do have useful input, and bring new ideas'. However he does work closely with his partner Nurit Israeli, who is involved throughout the process, and who explores computer applications to put together a home studio. Alkabetz credits her greater patience as a counterbalance to the frustration engendered by his own tendencies to self-criticism and perfectionism. Hence his current project, a pilot for an original TV series: 'Short, funny episodes that don't have to come from inner turmoil!'

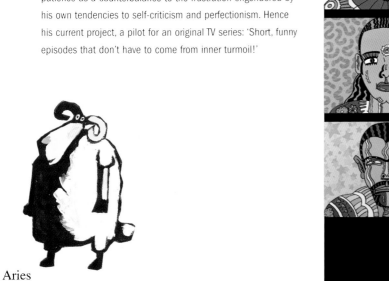

Aries

5

6

1

איור: גיל אלקבץ

2

Philip Hunt

From 3D to 2D

Pragmatism, and the need for constant creative stimulation, were decisive factors in model animator/director Philip Hunt's move to Studio aka, where he is now a partner and creative director. Having been hired by Barry Purves to work on Tim Burton's **Mars Attacks** for all of a week before it was decided to switch from stop-motion puppets to computer characters, he realised that he didn't have the level of output necessary to secure patronage for short films, and that his days were probably numbered as a model-animation director for commercials. Studio aka was keen to extend its range, and Hunt needed an environment where he could be creative, and keep his work changing all the time. He enjoys the speed and variety of the commercials industry, saying: 'At times it's like an extension of art school, you get to turn ideas around on a stick, and have to solve problems. I'd hate to have a single recognisable style, reinvention keeps the process fresh for me.' The studio has become an umbrella for diverse directorial talents ranging from the classically crafted to the stylistically idiosyncratic. It produces 2D, 3D, and stop-motion animation, as well as live-action, with every conceivable combination in between.

Hunt's role is initially to respond to advertising agency briefs, but also to encourage and cast the other directors. 'Often I might do a design pitch, but then pass it to another director because it needs a clear 2D approach. Sometimes we pitch out to the entire studio and everyone can input – including the runner and receptionist. I believe in pushing potential wherever it originates. It can simply be a matter of believing in someone, helping them move forward. We might pitch ten different routes and techniques or decide this isn't for us. I oversee things and make suggestions – something I also expect from the other directors on my own drawings and storyboards.' Hunt learned this reciprocal way of working from director Joan Ashworth in his early days in the industry.

The award-winning 'Orange' mobile phone network advertising campaign is an example of corporate work, which Hunt finds 'allows more creative leeway, unlike more "product" based advertisements, this is a brilliant incentive and perfect for pushing ideas in animation. The agency trusted their instincts and cast us for what we could achieve if given freedom, rather than what they thought they could tell us to do.' Hunt's initial stick drawing landed the first advertisement, and another eight followed, spread among him and the studio's other directors. Ironically, he would never have got it if the agency had realised he'd made the extraordinarily inventive William Burroughs' adaptation **Ah Pook is Here**. 'They'd seen it, liked it, but put me on the "no" pile. Way too weird!' By the time they did make the connection, however, they were more than happy with his work.

1

2

The tendency to pigeonhole people was why the studio preferred sending out the company reel to support a design pitch, rather than individual showreels. This 'allowed someone to be judged on their pitch, and not by what they'd done before'. The success of the first advertisement led the agency to trust them, 'so we could involve several animators who'd previously worked in more conventional animation. They might not have been considered for the advertisements based on their existing showreels and in some cases they didn't have one.'

Hunt feels computers seem to have unleashed a whole new wave of creativity. 'Five to ten years ago many animators weren't interested, and most were sceptical, with good reason. There's a big difference between animating in CGI and moving things about in SGI – for example, the difference between flying logos and **Toy Story**. However, now we're really seeing something exciting happen – Marie Paccou and Richard Kenworthy's films for instance. I would prefer to use a computer as a super-photocopier to do things I could never have dreamed of doing within the limitations of model animation, but still keeping it hands-on and low-tech, rather than trying to emulate feature film standards of production.'

3

(1–3) Early stop-motion model animation student films: Brecht adaptation **The Beggar and the Dead Dog** and children's film **Spotless Dominoes**.

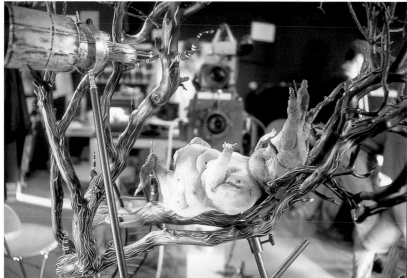

1

2

3

Hunt believes that 2D has had a resurgence after the late '80s set-back from the then popularity of innovative model animation, proving that pencil and paper is still a powerful and emotive form. 'I don't think stop-motion is dead – look at Aardman – but a lot of its commercial applications have disappeared. It's 3D that has had to grow to match these traditional standards.'

Studio aka has developed interactive internet games from the commercials the studio has produced. While researching a website for the studio, the studio saw some interesting experiments by web designers at Edwards Churcher Ltd., which sparked three collaborative projects with their studio for Compaq which won a D&AD award. They can be seen at www.studioaka.co.uk

'The internet is reinventing the way animation is thought out and has the potential to challenge conventional applications of animation. As an advertising medium it's still at kindergarten level. Who wants to look at banner commercials, and those annoying things that pop up with most internet advertising, or spend time downloading a soap commercial in QuickTime? But if there's something which engages your interest...'

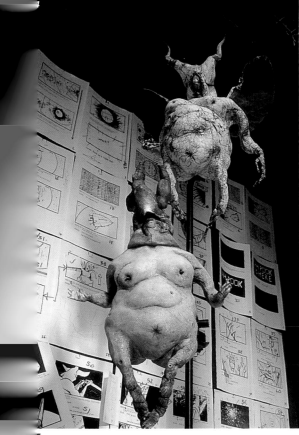

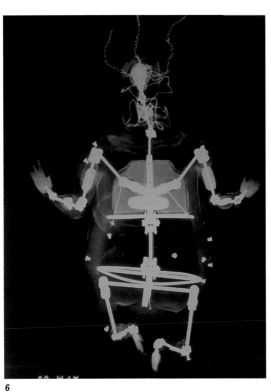

(1–6) Ah Pook is Here was
inspired by recordings of
Burroughs' live performance-
readings. 'The film's three parts
are drawn from a number of
books and performances from
different eras, which got me
through the door with Burroughs,
since that's what he'd always
done – cut-ups. He liked the
outline: the ideas, context and
drawings.' The final film prompted
Burroughs to ask Hunt to make
another. 'Ah Pook is Here was
very quickly and brutally made
and I think it was one of the
most direct and to-the-point
things I've done.' *(1–2)*
Production stills; *(3)* Hunt
and lighting cameraman Phillip
Timme; *(4–5)* models for Ah
Pook and his alter-ego puppet
and *(6)* X-ray of Ah Pook
armature body designed and
created by Mackinnon &
Saunders together with
Philip Hunt.

6

5

1   3

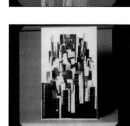

2   5

4

6

(1–17) Commercials for Orange. (1–6) Hills: (1–3) Concept drawings for original stick-man 'Larry Shortlegs'; (4) Mac test for mountains; (5) original set elements: a paper tree, wood splinters for mountains and cardboard for buildings and (6) images from the finished commercial. (7–8)The ad campaign not only increased sales but also generated fan mail. (9–12) Freewheeler:

(9) Pitch-work drawings. 'Larry Shortlegs had to ride a bike, but his legs were too short, so I gave him a scooter'; (10) storyboard; (11) still and (12) artwork for **Freewheeler** and **Hills** landscapes. The paper edges of books were photocopied. For **Hills** the elements were Mac-scanned and composited in Quantel Henry. In **Freewheeler** the photocopies were cut and shaped, then shot on film under rostrum in separate elements before compositing.

7

8

Inital ideas for 'Freewheeler'. The character (Larry)

9

1. Open on STICKMAN gliding through traffic. He waves hello

2. Puople look at him, we PULL OUT to see he is riding a scooter.

3. He heads off for a carefree ride into the country, waving the city behind

4. Passing by trees, he looks happy.

PAUL VAUGHN: ORANGE. BELIEVE A MOBILE PHONE SHOULD BE THE MOST RELIABLE THING YOU EVER USE

5. A dog tries to keep up.

6. But stops as he dips over a hill.

10

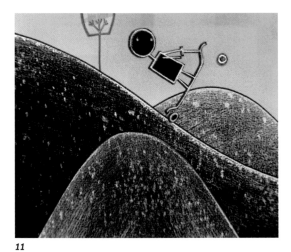

11

12

16

17

13

14

15

(13–17) **Megalomaniac** is an example of moving between 2D and 3D: The script specified a 'Blowfeld' type character in a Bond pastiche. 'We originally planned him in very stylised 3D. The 2D sketches worked, but the agency hated it in 3D. So we used the 2D rough sketches but animated full on and in a deliberately messy way – which initially mortified our classically-trained 2D animator Darren Vandenberg! But then he really got into it. The backgrounds deliberately subverted what computers are supposed to do, the boiling scratchy mess celebrates the pre-clean-up stage of animation drawings. Scanning the characters directly into the CGI, within a 3D "set", made the 2D character convincingly inhabit the space, virtually projected onto an invisible surface, and even casting a shadow.' (13) CGI test in 3D set test. (14) The character's development as he was put in the set. 'The rendering was done in greyscale using the Softimage programme to concentrate on the shapes, as colour was a separate concern and at this resolution was distracting. The screens were ultimately eliminated and his coat changed from white to black. The chair and console were also roughed up.' (15) 2D in 3D, second test by Andy Staverly. (16) Mega and the assistant. (17) 'Part of a thumbnail storyboard, usually done on the spot in a client meeting. This is pretty close to the final ad but due to the positioning of the voiceover information, the idea had to be trimmed down to fit the 30 second length.'

For now, commercials satisfy Hunt's urge to make things move, although paradoxically he'd also like to illustrate children's books. 'Ideally, I'd like to do a series or book for children which would come out at the same time as another film, darker and more surprising than **Ah Pook is Here**. In the end, short films have a certain kudos, the nearest you might get to leaving a piece of art behind, but for me, it would have to be from an absolute need to produce one.'

'Given all the heartache and agony involved in making animation, asking "why do it?" is like asking "why choose to spend four hours in the kitchen cooking a meal when you can slam something in the microwave?" It tastes better. Why not just draw, or build a model? Why isn't that enough? I want to see it move, I want to see it live all the clichés, but ultimately, it's always worth the wait. It's a way of single-handedly being able to create something. Having an audience respond to you without having to go out and speak to them and sometimes influencing the thoughts in the room is an incredibly powerful and seductive thing.'

1

2

3

(1–9) Commercial for Orange. **Megalomaniac:** (1) Part of later storyboard by Marc Craste; (2) test animation drawing by Darren Vandenberg; (3) mountaintop hideout concept: illustration done by Alan Kerswell; (4–9) images from the finished commercial.

4

7

5

8

6

9

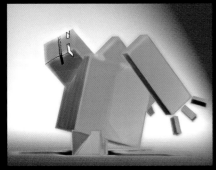

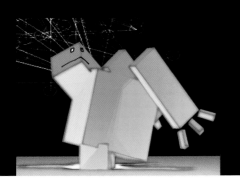

1

3

2

(1–3) Other commercial work.
(1) Ad for a bank: This is a combination of 2D and 3D computer graphics and shows a confrontation between a good robot – representing the bank, and the rest of the banks which are seen as cranky old rusty machines. The style is very illustrative and lo-fi. It is a 40 second ad and takes place in a weird and abstracted cityscape.
(2–3) Storyboards from a Coca-Cola commercial.

56

Philip Hunt

1. Open as darkness lifts over an industrial landscape.

2. Light flares as camera tracks through oil wells and pumps.

3. The oil field is an impressive sight.

4. The machines are like strange creatures.

5.

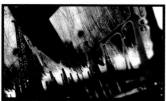

6. A flame flickers at the top of a well

7. We track in on the Well as the flames become more ferocious

8.

9. As we zoom right in on the flame a transformation takes place...

10. The Oil Well becomes longer and straighter.

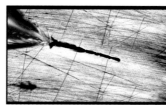

11. The sky now becomes the ground and the Oil well a missile.

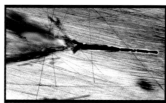

12. Camera twists and turns over the landscape with the missile

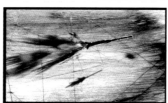

13. The missile shadow chsases along the terrain below.

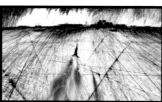

14. A city is seen in the distance.

15. The missile accelerates toward it

16.

17. camera overtakes missile and takes on P.O.V

18.

19. camera crash zooms into buildings

20. explosion and white out.

21.

22. TV static.

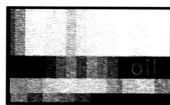

23. 'oil' logo appears over testcard.

24. super: step out of your world.
Red line resolves 'oil' logo.

(1–4) Commercial for an international magazine, **Oil Story**: 'The agency creatives wanted the ad to have a short sharp impact, to counter the magazine's conservative image. The script specified an oil well becoming a missile that destroys a city. The initial idea with a few key frame sketches got them intrigued – and brave enough to push me further. As time was very tight, I drew it all out in 25 pictures, using Photoshop to cut and paste elements into a coherent storyboard. To build a city at the end, I used some scanned paint textures and "found" a design by playing around with simple filters and processing in Photoshop. What began as an expedient time-saver quickly developed into the process of actually styling the ad. I wouldn't have drawn it that way with pencil and paper, but the time pressure can focus your creativity.'

Realising its raw look was just right for the project, the trick was then 'how to make that real and dimensionalise it.' Bram Tweam built the 3D version and Gary Brown composited the elements to Hunt's designs. They used a high-end CGI machine to build it in 3D, but deliberately kept camera angles simple and the models simple and crude. 'Composited on an expensive Henry, it was more polished than the storyboard, yet retained that raw lo-fi quality. It was a chance to test doing something quite abstract, low-tech and low-resolution in a way which would also feel believable.'
(1–3) Three storyboards from various stages of production.
(4) Stills from the finished commercial.

1/2/3

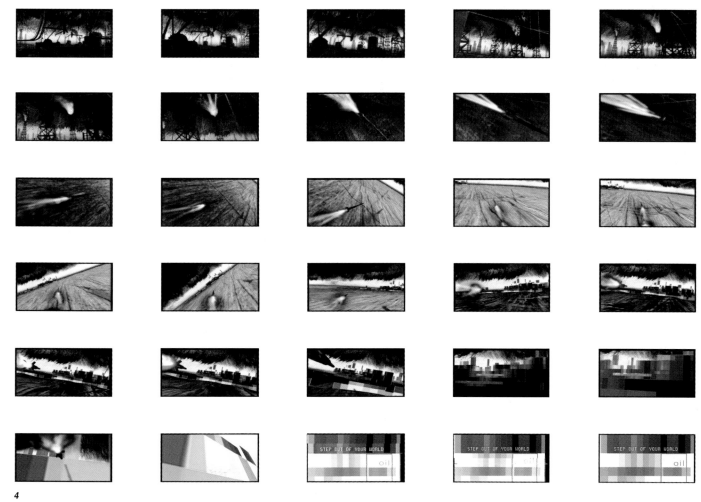

4

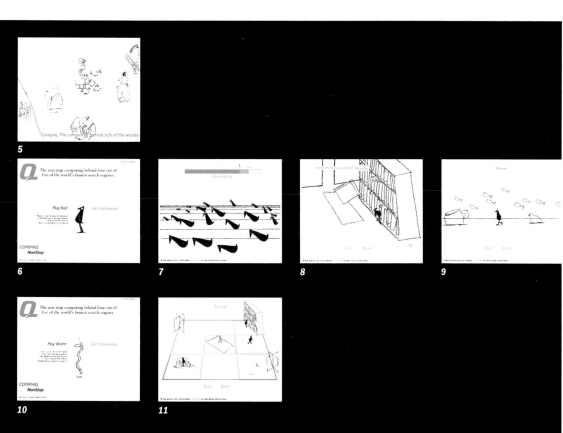

5

6

7

8

9

10

11

(5–11) Compaq interactive games was supervised by Hunt for Studio aka: (5) 'For the first interactive version of the game, the original artwork and animation from the **Hole in the Wall** ad was split so all the levels were independently controllable. Moving your mouse moves the character in real time, with no delay or obvious computer feel to it – like you're redirecting the ad. But unlike a 40 second ad, it's fun to play with for quite a while. (6–9) The search engine ad, with the bird looking for the worm which is in a different place each time, was perfect for a game-like structure. New animation sequences were done to walk the character in certain directions and with Edwards Churcher Ltd. we linked four of the ad's scenarios via software design and programming developed by James Stone, and simplified it to allow for current download times. (10–11) The last version makes you the worm evading the bird and was created purely for the internet.' The animation directors were Mic Graves, Dominic Griffiths, Mario Cavalli and Grant Orchard, who was also the designer.

Wendy Tilby

Collaborative filmmaking

Wendy Tilby discusses the genesis and evolution of her work, particularly in relation to **When the Day Breaks**, a National Film Board of Canada production, which she co-directed with Amanda Forbis. 'Originally I wanted to make an abstract film to music based on the concept that we are more than the sum of our parts. We are not merely a collection of physical parts such as limbs, cells and synapses, for it is our thoughts, our memories, our mothers – even our groceries – which truly define us. Our bodies are made up of bones and vessels and electrical currents like the buildings and pipes and wires which compose cities. But as with organisms, a city is not defined by its infrastructure but also by its inhabitants or its "life". I was inspired, in part, by Socrates who took for granted a kind of anatomical connection between individuals and their society – that our community is to each of us like a shared arm.'

These notions evolved into a narrative which, like Tilby's film **Strings**, uses physical connections such as plumbing as a means, or metaphor, to talk about connections or relationships with one another. In **Strings** Tilby was interested in the intimacy of urban lives: where individual existences are physically close, connected by walls, ceilings and pipes, but people often remain strangers. In the animation a man and a woman live in apartments one above the other in a residential block. Until a leaking bath brings them into direct contact, their relationship is one of encounters in the elevator, him hearing her bath running, her enjoying his music. Tilby wanted to suggest they are content with the symbiosis of this relationship and that when they actually meet, something alters, maybe irreversibly. There is a possibility of a 'relationship', certainly their next encounter in the elevator will be different. What if they prefer things the way they were?

A car accident is the catalyst in **When the Day Breaks**. Living in Montreal near a dangerous corner, Tilby would sometimes hear the squeal of tires, wait for the inevitable crash and wonder if someone was injured or dead: dwelling on the fact that someone's life – their body and their history – could be gone in an instant. And that someone else would soon discover they'd lost their loved one.

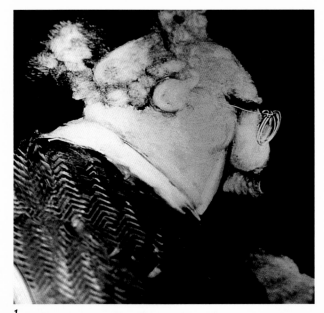

1

2

3

4

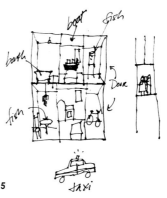

5

After studying
literature and writing Tilby took
filmmaking at art school, thinking
documentaries would synthesise
her writing and photography
interests. She became interested
in animation there, 'mainly
because of the solitary nature of
the process, the control; and I
loved to draw and paint. However,
I found it difficult and onerous
and nearly quit. Discovering paint
on glass kept me going. The
simplicity was attractive – you're
only concerned with the image in
front of you. No levels, no

tracing – and no going back.
The "straight-ahead" aspect of it
kept the perfectionist in me in
check. I also loved the texture
and messiness.'

'With **Strings** I wanted to use the
technique differently from in my
previous film, and from what
Caroline Leaf had so masterfully
achieved. I conceived of the
film almost as a tableau and
imagined the characters moving
within it almost as cut-outs.
No metamorphosis or animated
transitions. Camera moves were
done as table moves.'

The animation is about an accident as witnessed by
someone else. 'That the characters were strangers was
important... so I had them physically collide just prior to the
accident to establish this and also to implicate the protagonist
(the pig) in his (the chicken's) demise. Cause and effect. It
suggests she might feel guilty for bumping into him, delaying,
rattling or distracting him. A key image at this point was of a life
(physical and intangible) strewn out on the road – groceries, hat,
glasses, bones, cells, teeth, family, memories, experiences.
Another was of the lemon falling into the sewer grate, hinting
of things lost, of infrastructure, of the hidden world beneath the
street.' The poet John Donne wrote 'Any man's death diminishes
me, because I am involved in mankind; And therefore never send
to know for whom the bell tolls; it tolls for thee' – this was also
an influence for Tilby.

After numerous experiments with a variety of
under-camera techniques, Tilby discovered the potential of the
video printer and brought animator-filmmaker, Amanda Forbis, on
board as co-director of the project.

As visual experiments continued, the notion of the
film as musical developed and a three-part structure emerged.
Dennis Potter's use of optimistic Depression-era songs in **The
Singing Detective** was an influence. However, actual recordings
were problematic in terms of length and lyrics, so Judith
Gruber-Stitzer was enlisted to compose, and Forbis and Tilby
wrote the song lyrics.

A city versus country theme began to emerge. 'Initially,
the pig Ruby's view of the city is a very happy, positive one,
and this is underscored by the song; then her day is "broken"
by the tragic accident. A shot of blue sky and pastures after the
catalytic accident at the end of part two suggest the "happy
hunting grounds" or afterlife that the chicken has gone to – or
the pig's nostalgia for her rural roots. The city now appears
dangerous and hostile. Traumatised, Ruby rushes home and tries
to batten down the hatches, but triggered by her electric kettle,
her imagination travels through the connective tissue of the city
to the chicken's empty apartment as he might have left it that
morning, and out via his toaster.'

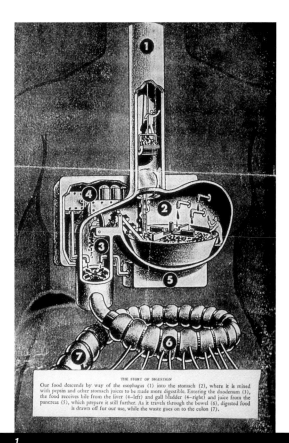

THE STORY OF DIGESTION

Our food descends by way of the esophagus (1) into the stomach (2), where it is mixed with pepsin and other stomach juices to be made more digestible. Entering the duodenum (3), the food receives bile from the liver (4–left) and gall bladder (4–right) and juice from the pancreas (5), which prepare it still further. As it travels through the bowel (6), digested food is drawn off for our use, while the waste goes on to the colon (7).

1

(1–10) When the Day Breaks:
(1) 'A family medical guide used to fascinate my sisters and me. Every major body system was illustrated as a mechanical one: for example, "The Story of Digestion" here. Such images influenced my thinking of an organism as city or city as organism.'

(2–6) 'I first tried under-camera techniques – ink and grease pencil on glass. The woman's house was drawn almost as a box (like a heart or other internal organ) with the connecting pipes and wires visible. I saw the city almost as a character, and portrayed it as schematics and cross-sections.'

(2–3) 'The characters were initially designed as fairly naively drawn humans. The female, a 30-something woman in the city, was problematic – females are much easier to do when children or elderly! **(7–8)** Thinking of David Hockney's exploded views of people and landscapes led to working with characters as deconstructed parts, trying to keep them in line with the theme. Characters were composed out of drawn bits on cel – and animated by replacing cel bits with different parts or positions. This was abandoned as too unwieldy and distracting to the story.'

2

3

4

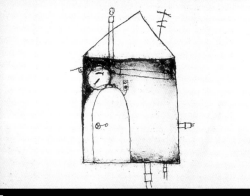

5

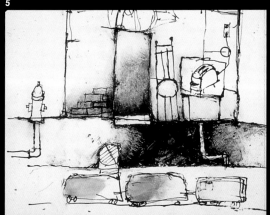

6

7

8

(9-10) 'We then started deconstructing characters and various actions, animating them separately on cut-out cel "boxes". For example: toast popping up, a lemon rolling and a milk bottle all were to be shown at once but in separate frames. This worked conceptually, but was impossible to execute without a computer.'

'The video printer was a great discovery, as selected frames were printed out – in boxes. The photographic realism lent substance to the characters and the city. The image could then be obliterated or retained and painted over, giving a lively, "boiling" effect. Disliking the rotoscoped look, we strived for a more jerky or abbreviated action where possible but were still unsure how to use this technique with the characters.'

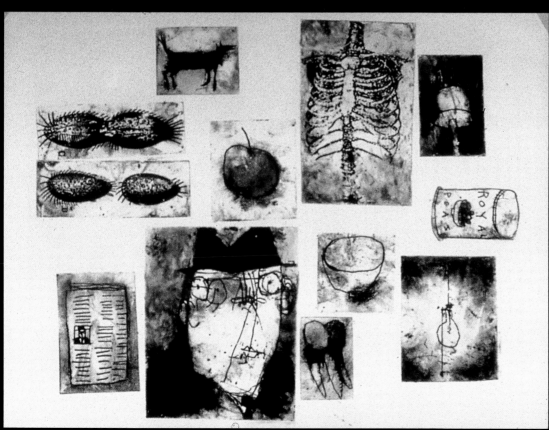

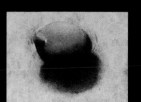

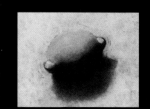

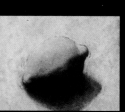

9

MR. C?

2

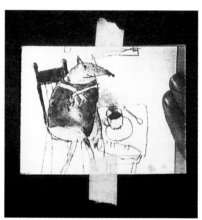

3

4

(1–5) **When the Day Breaks**:
A radical but liberating turning
point was making the characters
animals, who instantly became
more engaging and fun to work
with: particularly the protagonist
– infinitely more interesting (and
ageless) as a pig! Hence the
gleeful potato peeling.

5

'Along the way she feels her connection to the life of the
city, and this culminates in the final subway sequence. The
wistful song about the country, "Prairie Blue", evokes nostalgia
for innocent and rural pasts as the viewer moves through the
guts of the city. The motif of the subway sounds underscores
this. Rumbling at the film's start as the viewer emerges from the
blackness beyond the wall and follows the cord to the chicken's
toaster, it suggests the frightening unknown, the potential for bad
things behind the walls, beneath the streets, and under the skin.
It recurs over the sewer grate after the accident and finally when
we actually see the subway. Here, because the sound coincides
with the image of the subway, it is demystified. Ruby has
explored the subterranean, is able to eat her peels and
open her window shade. It should be clear that she is, at
the end of the film, a sadder but wiser pig.'

The starting points for Wendy are small visual moments
which she weaves into a concept or narrative, for example
here, a life strewn out on a road. They are usually imagined
observations and often have a strong sound component such
as music, sirens or water drops... The story and technique are
developed haphazardly by much trial and error and the order is
found from the chaos created. 'I have little compunction about
ditching stuff – even if it took weeks to create – a crazy way to
work with animation.'

Tilby believes 'the most interesting part of the process
is the conceptualising – a combination of writing, drawing,
painting and gathering – when everything is possible.
Because of the haphazard way I work, conceptualising and
tedious slogging phases alternate throughout production –
maybe this keeps things interesting. I like working on picture
and sound simultaneously as they feed off each other. This is
more possible now with access to digital editing, but generally,
I've had to complete the final picture cut before going on to
sound editing, music and foley, which I hated. Sound is probably
the most exciting stage because it can change everything. It's
like having a blood transfusion! Shots which seemed stale or
unworkable can suddenly have life and meaning breathed
into them. Foley is particularly fun and a good dose of instant
gratification, sorely needed in those final stages. As my films
to date are wordless, I'd love to do something that starts
with sound – music or words. An imposed structure can be
extremely liberating.'

1

2

3

4

5

6

7

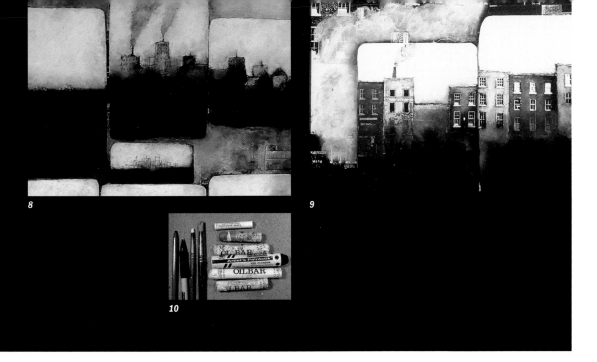

8
9

10

(1–13) When the Day Breaks:
(1–7) Friends as actors – and
the city – were shot on Hi-8,
then transferred to VHS. Video
prints were selected and
photocopied onto paper, with
pencil and oil sticks used on top.
Tilby comments: 'This process is
very enjoyable. I'm not tempted
to go back to paint on glass!' The
difficulty was that the artwork
was both very small (4 x 5
inches) and fully painted. As it
is impossible to paint two frames
exactly the same way, the
variation in the line and texture
from one frame to another causes
a 'boiling' or 'flicker' effect. At
best, the flicker is lively and
interesting. At worst, it's messy
and distracting. **(8–9)** Rendering
wide-shots was difficult, and the
rather claustrophobic effect of all
the close-ups was countered by
showing cityscapes almost as

11

snapshots in the title sequence.
(11–12) This 'moving snapshot'
effect is used again in the elegiac
'life of the chicken' sequence.
(11–14) 'I've never succeeded
in properly scripting or
storyboarding. It's always a
combination of drawings,
thumbnail storyboards and
shot lists. Everything is open
for change – additions,
subtractions, revolutions – until
the last possible moment.
(This can be very exasperating
for collaborators.)'

PART 2
RUBY SURVEYS GROCERIES
AND COMPONENT PARTS
OF CHICKEN'S LIFE.

12

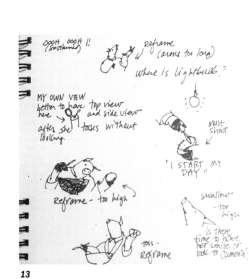

13

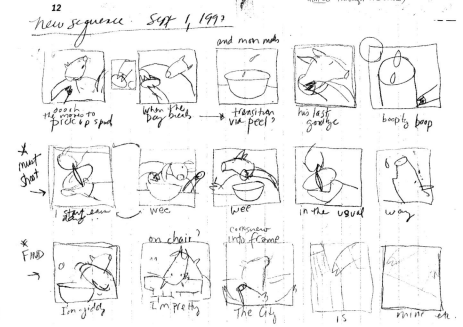

14

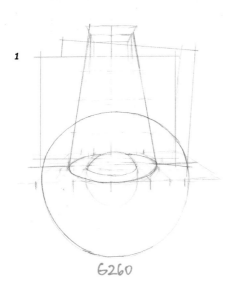

1

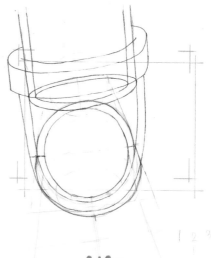

New 1

G260   G197

3

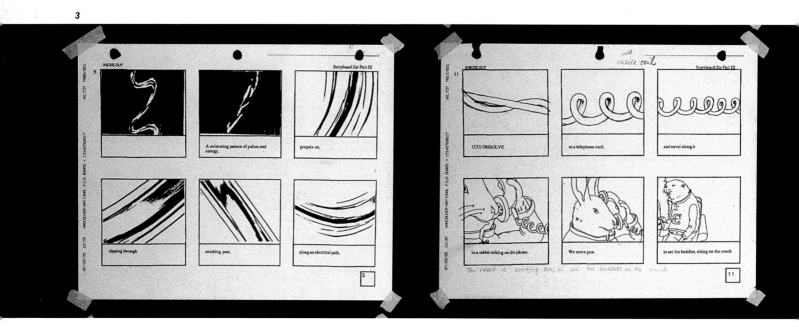

(1–10) **When the Day Breaks:**
(1–2) A lemon going through the sewer, first as a diagram, and then rendered. *(3)* Martin Rose's storyboard for the black and white 'pipes and wires' sequence in the third part. He designed and animated, drawing with pencil on paper – then filmed on 35mm and reversed into negative on computer. *(4–5)* Martha Wainwright and Chaim Tannenbaum recording the music; *(6)* Amanda Forbis, Tilby's co-director.

4   5   6

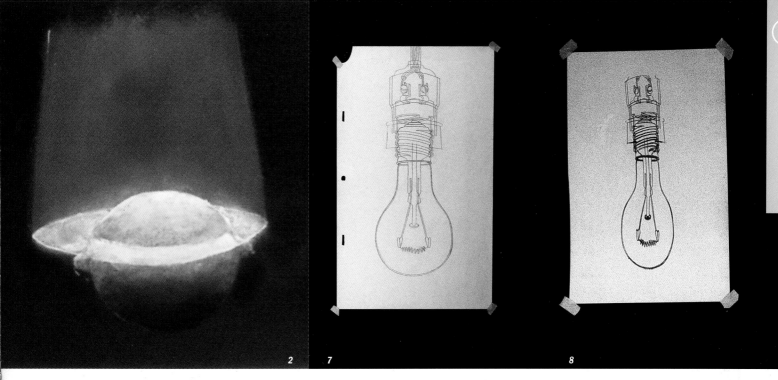

2

7

8

'Having worked solo on the first two films, collaborating with Amanda was a big – but welcome – change. Brainstorming together was always exhilarating. We are very like-minded and have a similar sense of humour and aesthetics. We would, of course, occasionally lock horns and have to negotiate our differences in style or opinion. For me, these difficulties were minor and more than made up for by Amanda's tremendous contribution and commitment to the project – and the comfort of having a cohort there in the trenches with me! It also made dealings with other collaborators easier: we could stand our ground more firmly together than either of us could solo.'

Tilby doesn't consider traditional craft skills to be the most crucial element of animation filmmaking. 'Ideas, a sense of timing, structure and aesthetic coherence are all important to me.' Her influences are not so much animation as short stories, moments in feature films, painting, graphic arts, photography, music and science, though she does cite three favourite animations: Gianluigi Toccafondo's **La Pista**, Caroline Leaf's **Metamorphosis of Mr Samsa**, and Ed Ackerman's **Primiti Too Ta**. For Amanda Forbis, 'as a dormant cut-out animator, I am deeply influenced by Yuri Norstein's work, so was particularly delighted by Eugene Fedorenko and Rose Newlove's **The Village of Idiots**. I also love the work of Gil Alkabetz, Priit Pärn, Caroline Leaf, the Fleischers and Zlatko Grgic.'

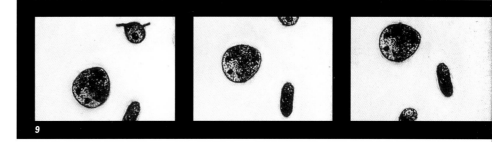

9

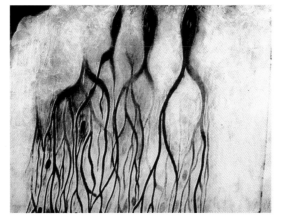

10

(7–8) A lightbulb, drawn then distorted slightly on the photocopier. *(9)* For the chicken's 'soul departing' sequence *(see also previous page, 12)*, images of body cells were photocopied from a medical book and animated as cut-outs under the video camera linked to the printer. The print-outs were then painted and filmed as a cycle. *(10)* Photocopied blood vessels, painted and moved under the camera.

Igor Kovalyov

From Russia to Hollywood

American animation studio Klasky Csupo, named after its Hungarian and American founders, has brought a distinctive new look to mainstream American cartoons, with series such as **RugRats, Duckman** and **Aahh! Real Monsters**. This flair and vision led them to invite Russian animator-director Igor Kovalyov to join the studio, after seeing his mysterious, yet utterly compelling short films at festivals. In between work on the studio's commercial projects, he is encouraged to make his own films, and enjoys total artistic freedom. 'I never have to show anyone anything until the film is finished. All they need to know is the length, and how many people I need to work with me and the studio then allocates a schedule.'

Kovalyov finds relatively little difference between production methods in America and Russia, although he adds 'I have only worked at Klasky Csupo – which is very European'. Some of his closest collaborators from Russia are still with him, in particular three people he trusts and always works with: Zhenia Delioussine, Andrei Svislotsky and Dima Malanitchev; 'They are amazing artists, and always understand me'. Kovalyov's next studio project is an adult feature adaptation of a Bukowski novel, The Way the Dead Live, for cable TV, which he will co-direct with a Hungarian animator and an almost entirely Russian crew.

The starting point for his own films is usually, 'just one small detail', maybe a single sketchbook drawing, or an almost imperceptible gesture glimpsed on television. If this detail has emotional resonance and lingers in his mind, he knows he's ready to start making something. 'It's like a snowball, starting from one snowflake. If I've forgotten it, after a week, a month, then I'm not ready.' Development is always a different, and very long process. 'Sometimes, the detail gets lost in the big snowball, and I can only see it when the film is done, sometimes it becomes the main idea, or the film's most important scene. It's like a very big and complicated puzzle, which I work through step by step. Sometimes I'm not sure about the script until the last piece fits into the puzzle. When I feel a certain harmony, then I start working on timing.' It's only then that Kovalyov realises how long the film will be. As he's writing, he feels impelled to tell his story to someone. 'I can't be quiet, I really need a reaction or opinion. Sometimes I get new, fresh ideas from that person, but sometimes a negative response can confirm your own instincts. It's the process that's important.' He only feels ready to start

1

drawing once the script is finished, saying that, 'when writing, I can visualise everything, but it's all in my head'. He designs almost all his characters and backgrounds, but the designer Malanitchev is responsible for colour and texture. Unusually, Kovalyov's scripts contain very detailed action and timing instructions; he never storyboards for his own films, relying on the detailed script to start working directly on the layout. 'I have to be very organised before I do layout and animation – although I can always change things when I see pencil tests.'

2

(1–2) Stills from **Andrei Svislotsky**: Kovalyov's most personal film, drawn from memories of childhood summers spent in the family's country house in Kiev. 'A certain atmosphere – details that stayed in my mind, the strange relationship between a couple of men...' The fact that it is named after one of his close collaborators was simply because Kovalyov wanted a title that sounded Polish.

(3–6) Stills from **Bird in the Window**: An influence on Malanitchev's design for this film was one of his favourite painters, Klimt, which can be seen in the architectonic design and the rich colours. Generally, however, Kovalyov prefers a more monochromatic palette.

3

4

5

6

1

2

3

ANIMATION	SOUND
Sc. # 88 BG # 88 Frames 40-41	
CLOSE UP - MIDDLE.	
Jacob looks in the camera (sad eyebrows). The top of the frame slightly cuts his head, the lower part of the frame _ chest level (maybe slightly higher). Jacob looks in the camera (4 frames), then closes his eyes fast (2-3 frames). 5 whole frames with closed eyes. After that Jacob falls (from the camera) back disappearing behind the frame. This movement takes 19 frames, 10 whole frames of the background only.	Bertha's quick steps (O.S.)
Sc. # 89 BG # 89 3.7-3.9 sec	
MIDDLE SHOT.	
Jacob lies on the bed, head to the right, the frame cuts on his knees on the left. Jacob pulls the blanket on. In the first frame of this scene the blanket is at the level of Jacob's neck, by the end of the scene he pulls the blanket over his head, then his arms holding the blanket pull further and he stretches them by the sides of the pillow. The movement is slow, the scene ends still in motion (no whole frames). From the beginning to the very end of the scene: slow PAN from left to right.	Bertha's steps fade out (O.S.)
Or, maybe, the arms with the blanket stop, but PAN continues to the end of the scene. Beginning to end - 70 frames. Fade out - 7 frames.	After fade out on the black frame Bertha's shuts the door.

4

5

His animators rarely read the complete script and so never know how the film will look in the end, they simply follow his direction. 'Zhenia Delioussine often says when he's working, he's not interested in knowing, and prefers to see it when it's finished, with sound.' Igor explains what the characters are doing using drawings and key poses, and he gives the timing; sometimes with a degree of latitude, but on particular scenes, very exactly. 'If I need a new perspective, I deliberately only explain what I need for that scene and the animator does the poses himself. The timing, however, is mine alone.' When doing layout he occasionally finds he can't stop himself animating, leaving only the in-betweens to be done.

(1–4) **Bird in the Window**:
(1–3) Stills; (4) script extract.
(5–7) Sketchbook drawings.
'Lots of ideas from those books and drawings I put into my films.'

'In pre-production, I have to be sure about everything. Production is just a physical process, I don't have to think, just follow what I've already planned. They're both very hard. You have to work like crazy, mentally and physically. Only at post-production do I feel like a director. I'm instructing my colleagues, because I've already decided at an earlier stage what I want for sound and cuts, so I just explain what I need.'

For Kovalyov, sound is as important as action. Sometimes he can only envision an action to a particular sound. Sound in his films is often off-screen. 'I usually make a special rhythm with the sound, for me it's like music.' His use of actual music is very sparing, and invariably occurs at the end of the film, for example the snatch of Turkish song in **Bird in the Window**, or the Japanese flute in **Andrei Svislotsky**, chosen entirely for emotional resonance.

6

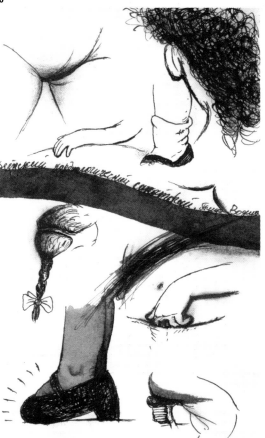

7

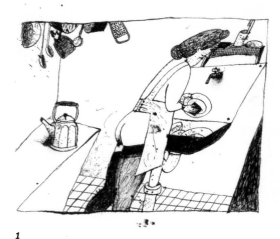

1

2

Осенью 1938 года в этом доме проф. Вавилов был прикован к постели тяжёлой болезнью.

Дочь Тася и жена Татьяна до последнего были рядом с больным учёным.

3

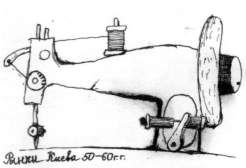

4

5

(1–7) Sketchbook drawings.

7

Although Kovalyov had drawn constantly from early childhood, he could not get into art college. However, when a friend introduced him to a studio in Kiev, he immediately recognised his vocation saying, 'In my drawings I'd always been trying to move my characters, giving them lots of different poses'. After working at the studio as in-betweener and ink-and-painter, then graduating via rigorous tests to the animation class, he was offered an unconditional place on a new course in Moscow for animator/directors.

The move to the metropolis was a revelation. His studies included literature, philosophy and cinema, with Norstein and Tarkovsky amongst his teachers, and it was an intensely stimulating period. Seeing films on a big screen that he'd only previously read about, he found his major influences. Apart from Polish animator Borowcyck, they were all live-action: Ingmar Bergman, Carl Dreyer, and Robert Bresson, whom he calls 'my teacher'. He vividly recalls the shock of seeing **Diary of a Country Priest** for the first time in 1978. 'It was a whole new world: the organic harmony of the film, the simple story, how the characters moved, the ideas.' It is important, for Kovalyov, that a film 'creates a world I feel I can recognise, but only if it's not a real world. When a film is very simple, it turns into something different. I can believe it; the situation feels like a dream, very natural.' Among younger filmmakers, he admires Leos Carax, and in animation, feels a close affinity with the Quay Brothers, who also share his passion for Dreyer and Bresson.

1

2

3

(1–7) Stills from **Flying Nansen**: Kovalyov's own films are distinguished by his use of camera moves, which are often long, lateral pans across the scene and difficult to illustrate with still images. (5–7) Towards the end of **Flying Nansen** one such pan moves from a drawn scene across to a montage of Giotto frescoes to rest on one of Kovalyov's favourite paintings by this artist: the two monks' facial expressions mirror those of some characters in the film.

4

As a student, Kovalyov rebelled against the imposition of conventional narrative rules. He feels however that 'rhythmic structure is important' – hence the stress on timing in his scripts. The consequent sense of utter inevitability to what happens in the films gives them a powerful emotional impact, if one renounces the need to make conventional sense of them. 'I'm always afraid of trying to "say something". Different people have different interpretations. A film should generate lots of questions, but it should be organic. My theory is that any art, for example a painting, must touch you, but you don't have to understand it. I see the world as quite mysterious. What is the truth? Nobody knows.' Unsurprisingly, for Kovalyov, 'a film must first of all be interesting for me – and maybe also people whose taste is very close to mine. My theory is that a director has to make a movie for himself.'

He sees **Hen**, **His Wife**, **Andrei Svislotsky** and **Bird in the Window** as a trilogy in terms of style, design, and theme – and all draw on his own experience of life. 'You could say they are all about human loneliness and freedom, the gap between people. They're also about myself. If you are lonely, you are not free, and you're not free if you have problems with yourself or other people. Art is a way to be free, it's a kind of transcendence. Maybe it's banal, but it's like to be free means to be with God.'

Flying Nansen is rather different from his previous films – perhaps because its evolution differed from his usual pattern. Initially intending it to be more gag-oriented, Kovalyov then decided 'to tell a very simple story and to make it an exercise in drawing. It was the first time in my life that I didn't know how it would end when I started drawing; and when I started on layout, I didn't know what the last scene would be. It's difficult to say why I decided to change style. Maybe it's because I changed genre.'

'I've been doing animation all my adult life and I'm still learning. As for the future: it's a very scary question. Maybe when I'm very old, I would like to very quietly make some films for myself and not show them to anybody, since I'm pretty sure that the future of art is only for or with young artists.'

5   6   7

8

(8–10) Stills from the **RugRats** movie, co-directed by Kovalyov with Norton Virgien. The film's non-stop dialogue and frantic pacing is in total contrast to Kovalyov's own films. *(11–14)* Stills from TV series **Aahh! Real Monsters**.

Studio TV and film producer Gabor Csupo on his move to bring Igor to the studio: 'His style was totally different from what typical Hollywood TV productions require. But I just trusted in his talent – I thought that he could easily modify his skill and I was right.' Csupo originated the idea for the series **Aahh! Real Monsters,** and once the show had been greenlit by Nickelodeon, he showed them Kovalyov's films. The channel liked the design style, although it was too sophisticated for TV, but wanted to see what he'd come up with for the series. A pilot was made from just a two page script. 'In a complete reversal of the usual procedure, we made an animatic with rough dialogue and then the writers wrote dialogue from our storyboard', Csupo continues. 'Igor became one of the head directors and designers on the show. The look – all the colours, designs, layouts and shadows – was brought in by Igor and his colleagues Sergei, Dima, Andrei, Zhenia and Gena.'

9

10

11

12

13

14

Lejf Marcussen

Exploring visual ambiguity

'If we don't have the "superfluous", meaning those things that cannot save the world, then there is no reason to save the world. If you leave out love, because you want to save the world, then there is no point in saving it. There are too many people wanting to save the world who say, "first and foremost, we need information, then we can have the "superfluous", but love and art will be lost, if we leave it to the end.'

This comment from Danish filmmaker Lejf Marcussen gives some measure of the passion underlying his aesthetic position. He perceives two kinds of art: 'That which is programmatic or predictable, in that it tells you something you already know, or reinforces what you are supposed to know; and that which is not. That's the difference between art and illustration. In the Middle Ages art had to be narrative and dramaturgical, gradually over the centuries art has been able to free itself. Art is at its richest when it's not programmatic.'

Each of Marcussen's new films is a need to explore the medium's potential – although never as a vehicle for narrative. Hence each film looks different, often employing different techniques, some of which Marcussen has devised himself. However, as Italian critic Bruno di Marino points out, 'the transformations in his films, unlike those films which focus attention on their technique, draw attention rather to "the act of looking", and reflect an acute awareness of the ambiguity of vision'.

He was already drawing as a two-year-old and by the age of eight had 'instinctively' mastered perspective. There was no training in animation available when he studied graphics and then fine art, and so he taught himself. Marcussen found work at Danish TV in its very early days, when they needed artists to create visual interludes between programmes, and he was able to use the facilities there to learn and experiment.

For Marcussen, the very notion of a script is an anathema: 'I envy the spontaneity of painters and composers who can just take up their tools and work, without the need to envisage the result. That pure combination of yourself and your tools without a script to pre-determine the process.'

This working method means he never knows how long a film will be until it's finished, thus the sound comes after, with the exception of **Tonespor**, whose form came about through a happy accident: 'For many years I had been thinking about how counterpoint and polyphonic structure could be animated without betraying – and as such destroying – the music through illustration or the imposition of a narrative.' Marcussen realised that he could not attempt the animation of individual notes, as this would be too abrupt for the sensations they elicit. As a score is symbolic, he wanted the film to be more of an analogue. 'Then one day a piece of paper floated off the table and the play of the light through it gave me the idea: this was music.' He took a movement from a Carl Nielsen symphony and started making tests, using formations of lines coloured to represent different orchestral sections. The tests, using different speeds of animation to match the varying music speeds, were shown to people to see if they felt it fitted the feeling of the music. In every case they agreed on the speed being correct – although not necessarily on the colours he had chosen for the different instruments.

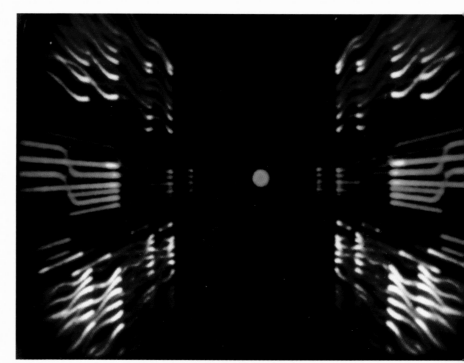

1

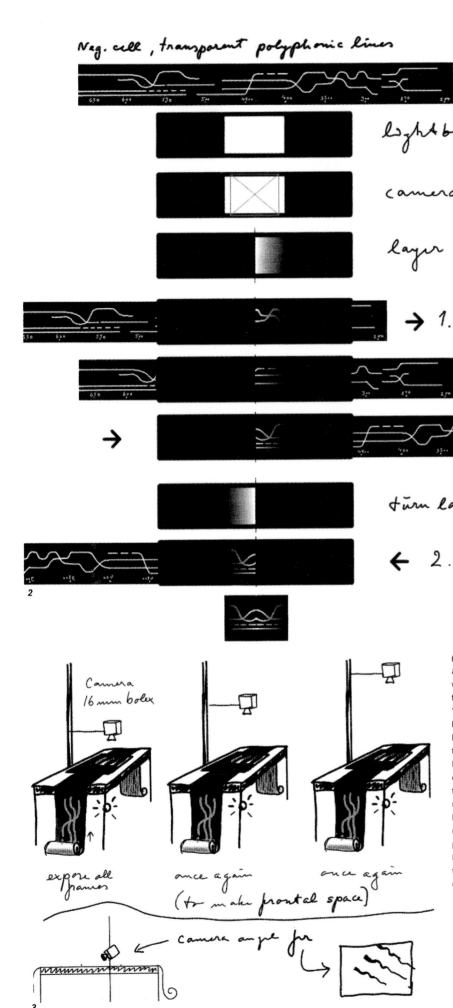

Neg. cell, transparent polyphonic lines

light box

camera

layer

→ 1. exp.

→

→

türn layer

← 2. exp.

2

Camera
16 mm bolex

expose all
frames

once again
(to make frontal space)

once again

camera angle for

3

(1–3) Tonespor: William Moritz, a specialist in abstract film and visual music, has described how the coloured lines are plotted, 'so they appear with a sharp bright attack then decay in a long fading line, just as musical tones do'. To obtain this effect, Marcussen realised that: 'The ear processes sound quicker than the eye does images, yet the ear needs to retain previous notes heard to make sense of it as music, so I had to find a "now" point to start the image, which had to be a little bit lighter than the next frame otherwise you couldn't connect it to the music.

I then had to fade to black.' Lines were painted black onto celluloid, the film was reversed to negative, and then the lines were coloured in to match the orchestral instruments. Each set of instrumental lines were shot several times using multiple exposures – 72,000 in all – winding the film back to build the sense of depth, so it appears almost 3D. The first four minutes of the film were three to four metres long, and the last 30 seconds were 25 metres.

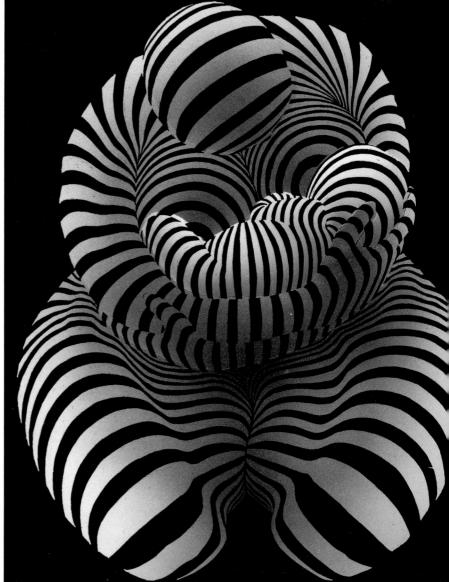

2

1

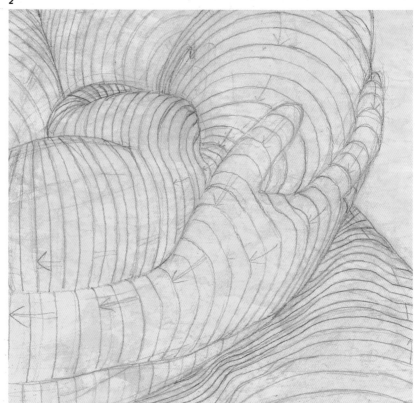

(1–3) Stills: The sculptural forms were drawn on cel with felt tip pen. Marcussen pencilled in arrows on his artwork as a guide to indicate the directions in which the lines were to move.

(4–9) The Public Voice: 'Churches and temples have always been designed in such a way as to enhance their purpose, and symmetry is a powerful element in this design. It reinforces their power and credibility (also symmetry is as far from nature as one can get). This has been the case from the most ancient times to this century – from Ptolemy's temple to both ordinary churches and the Nuremberg "set-design" created for Hitler by his architect Albert Speer. All are designed to focus attention on the priest, and amplify the voice.' **(5)** Drawing of the Delvaux painting which gives the film its title.

3

The film has been recognised by musicologists as a perfect visualisation of counterpoint. Ironically, this perfection is often assumed to be the result of using a computer. Yet, as Marcussen points out, 'no computer can distinguish between the lines of notes in polyphony, as when they connect there are two or three new sounds. The computer doesn't recognise this, but the human ear can.' **Tonespor** has been used in education, as a test to enable those labelled 'tone-deaf' to discover, through the visualisation, that they are not. Even those who knew that particular Nielsen piece very well told him they had never recognised the ambulance siren effect in the trumpets section until they saw the film.

His interest in creating 3D space on a 2D screen can be seen as early as in the figure of the orchestra conductor in **Lederkonkurrenz** (Master Competition). 'The idea was to use very minimal drawn lines and lighting effects from both sides, to see if I could get the audience to fill in the forms.' **Stills** further developed this exploration of spatial dimension. Marcussen wanted to see if it was possible to convey the sense of sculptural plastic form through 'still' images, instead of using animation to imitate the conventional live-action approach of moving the camera around a 3D object. The film was 'an empirical experiment, to see what would happen if I made the lines of the drawings move, to represent volume rather than shape'. He made the soundtrack as a conglomerate of recordings from an old shortwave radio, because, 'since you don't understand its meaning, you invent it, creating pictures in your head'. The film's challenge to 'programmatic art' provoked offical disapproval from the Eastern European delegation at a Hungarian TV festival during the Soviet regime. Although over the course of the festival, Marcussen was approached by several individuals from that delegation who furtively whispered how much they liked the film, but that it was not possible to say so in public. In the year following the fall of the Iron Curtain, the film was bought by almost every Eastern European country.

Some of the techniques he has devised still leave audiences awed and amazed today – in particular the extraordinary 'virtual zoom' effect of **The Public Voice**, which was in part prompted by dislike of the conventional film travelling zoom, where the fade from the old zoom to the new was too obvious, and, as such, distracting. The opposition of the film's two parts in a sense embodies his aesthetic. In the first, a series of framed paintings appear and a magnifying glass moves across them, breaking sections of the paintings down into structural diagrams as though to explain, and hence contain, these works of art – to 'master the picture'. Then, accompanied by menacing, bombastic music which underscores the impulse to impose order and meaning, the camera appears to go through, via what Marcussen calls a 'progressive zoom', an endlessly receding corridor in which architectural forms appear, typifying 'programmatic art'.

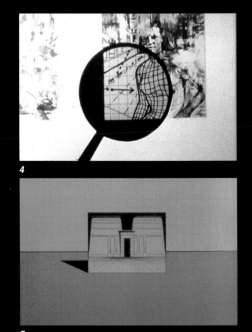

4

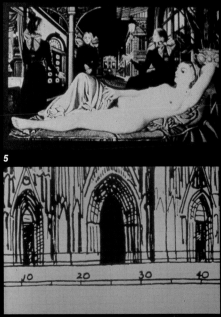

5

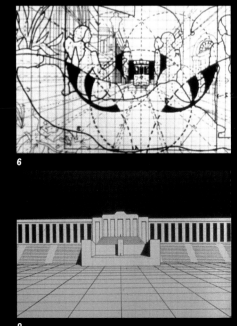

6

7

8

9

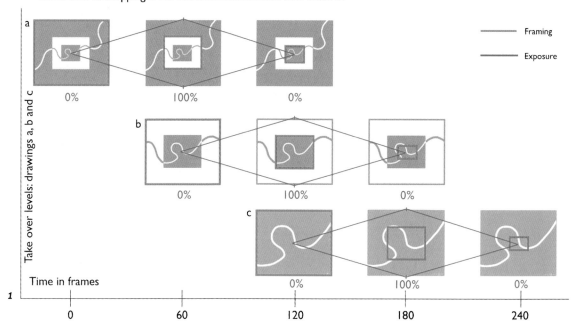

Three level overlapping cross-dissolve matched take-over track-in

— Framing
— Exposure

Take over levels: drawings a, b and c

a

0%   100%   0%

b

0%   100%   0%

c

0%   100%   0%

Time in frames

1

0   60   120   180   240

The second part of the film is an apparently seamless 'regressive' zoom out from a detail of Delvaux's painting, 'The Public Voice' as seen at the beginning of the film. The painting was chosen for the symmetry of the tram in the background, as a bridge from the symmetry of the architectural forms. As this detail recedes, it transforms to become the detail of another painting, and so on as the zoom continues through an unbroken series of virtuoso transformations. His soundtrack collages different musical sources, in particular Luciano Berio's 'Sinfonia', which is important to Marcussen for its Babel-like orchestration of vocal citations from Samuel Beckett's play The Unnameable. 'Beckett was concerned with how you can only think inside the established frames, for example of language, and the film is about the possibility of taking yourself outside these frames.' This theme is the reason for the opposition between the framed pictures in the first part and the removal of frames in the second through the zoom. Marcussen explains that 'the minute tone variations of the singing underscore the zoom effect'.

The succession of images – most of them recognisable from the history of Western art – in no way constitute an analytic or interpretative commentary on that tradition. The point, for Marcussen, was that the succession of paintings could not be determined or planned for in advance. 'It's the pictures themselves which make the pictures. I couldn't choose the forms, each picture determined the one that succeeded it.' Focusing on the silhouette of a form in one painting, he'd scan his memory for another painting in which a similar shape appeared, one which would maintain a rhythmic pace to the film. When he got stuck, he'd place the problematic picture at the end of his bed until it suggested the next.

Once again, it is generally assumed that the film was made with a computer, but it was in fact entirely drawn, and the only computer involved was that of an engineer Marcussen called upon to help calculate the tiny incremental exposure changes needed for his zoom effect.

Marcussen had hoped others might experiment with the principles involved in this technique, and found it ironic that instead he received calls from people saying, 'I have a good idea for using your zoom' – when in fact the principle was not to have a pre-determined idea.

He has always made his films virtually single-handed. His need to work empirically, and his rejection of scripts makes it difficult for him to work in contemporary TV, which he sees as regressive and fixated on the verbal. Marcussen feels that the internet may be the only chance for personal art. He is now experimenting with computers, which he feels have opened up fascinating new possibilities. He is excited by 'the idea of creating imaginary but convincing depth on an essentially 2D, flat surface'.

(1–2) The Public Voice: (1) Diagram of the technique used. With flat drawings on an animation rostrum, a zoom is made by incrementally (frame-by-frame) moving the camera towards or away from the artwork. Given the complexity of Marcussen's use of this technique for this film, a computer was used to calculate the amount of light required (i.e. frame 0, one per cent, two per cent etc.). This was done for each successive exposure, to give the effect of one zoom invisibly dissolving through into the next zoom.

(2 and continued on following pages) Artwork sequences from the film. Throughout the second section, the structure, i.e. the silhouette forms, remains constant, but the proportions of the two pictures are changing all the way through.

2

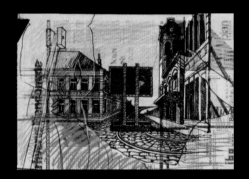

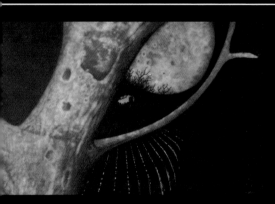

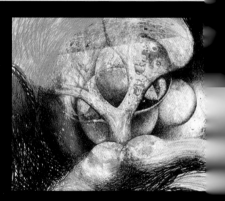

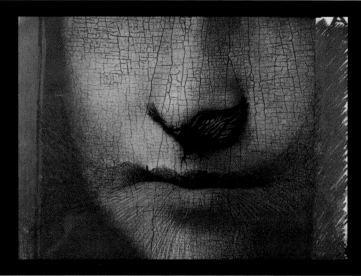

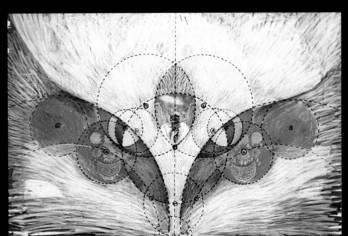

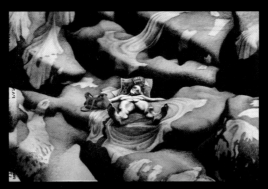

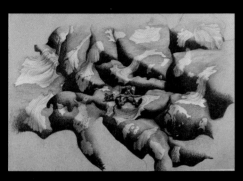
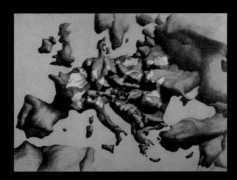
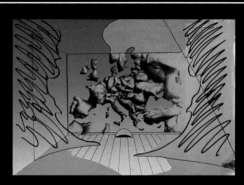

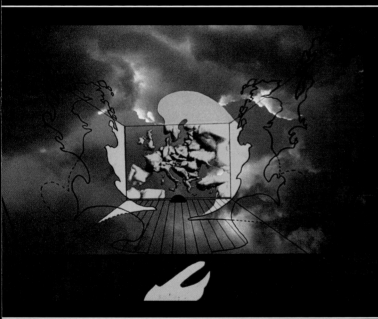

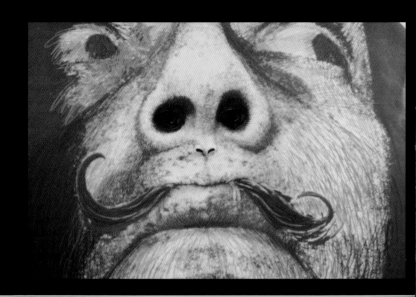

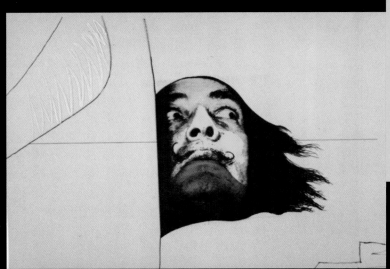

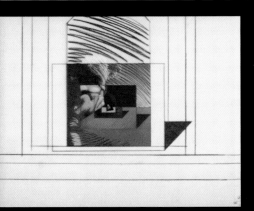

Piet Kroon

Processing the creative thought

Piet Kroon is currently animation co-director on **Osmosis Jones**, a combination live-action and animation feature film from Warner Bros., where he has worked as a storyboard artist for the last few years. Self-taught, Kroon studied film and theatre rather than going to art college. He observes, 'For a lot of animators the visual end is the purpose of their work. My main interest as a filmmaker, is in the narrative aspects.' After his first film, which he describes as, 'deeply meaningful, though you'd never know from watching it', he wanted his second, **DaDA**, to communicate. 'The most honest way to check if you're connecting with the audience is to try to make them laugh: it works, or it doesn't.' The film has no dialogue, which meant visual storytelling: finding and developing clear metaphors. **DaDA** was conceived by Kroon when working as an animator on **Waterpeople**, a film by Paul Driessen. Kroon admires Driessen for his ability to spin a whole film out of one core idea, either a central visual metaphor – for example, the different meanings a simple horizontal line can take on, or a formal film element that is explored, such as split-screen, sound or no sound, or positive and negative space.

The idea for DaDA was triggered by a campaign poster he once designed for over-burdened nurses, featuring a freaked out nurse, with an enormous pile of legislation and medical handbooks flattening her head. That sparked the notion of judging a man by the covers of the books on his head.

Kroon uses two different and simultaneous approaches to develop ideas. 'One is like "dreaming out loud", switching off one's rational side, letting it flow. By contrast the other – inspired by Stan Hayward's approach to writing for animation – is very logical and almost mathematical, involving lists and exhaustively exploring connections between the idea's components. With **DaDA**, for example: cookery books, gardening books, encyclopaedias, comics and such were listed; and different professions: clergy, lawyers, police etc. Or language – to throw the book at someone, bookworms and so on. Doodling can also generate visual lists: people with books on their head in different situations (cars would have to have a sunroof, what if it rains?). A lot of this ended up in the film. These two approaches can be complementary: the mathematical exercises can generate springboard material for "dream-quests". When a snowballing idea comes to a stop, there's a whole new set of components to analyse and explore.'

1

OHSLAAN.
KINDEREN LOPEN IN DE PAS NAAR SCHOOL.

CUT
EEN LEERLING HEEFT EEN BEURT VOOR DE KLAS.

OHSLAAN.
MENSEN LOPEN NAAR EEN KERK. ALLERLEI BOEKEN OP HUN HOOFD, BIJBEL ONDER HUN ARM.

CUT
EEN VRIJPARTIJ. EEN BEETJE BEDUUSD KIJKT MM WELK BOEK "ON HER MAN'S MIND" IS.

CUT
DD LUISTERT MET EEN GLAS AAN MM'S BUIK. MM KIJKT VERTEDERD HET SPOCK-BOEK DOOR.

CUT
TERWIJL DD ALS EEN BLIND PAARD DOORPEEST STRAAT MM OP OM HAAR BREIWERKJE TE PARKEN.

CUT
DD LUISTERT WEER AAN DE BUIK. MM BREIT NU IN VLIEGENDE VAART KINDERSOKJES...

2

3   4

5   6

(1-6) DaDA: (1) Two storyboard extracts; Kroon's storyboard drawing style was influenced by Paul Driessen, for whom Kroon worked as an animator at the time. However, for the film itself he opted for a more traditional cartoon style. 'Balance is a key idea in the film, in animation that means establishing a world with "real" gravity, where things have weight.' The Driessenesque elements which remained were the hilly landscape (hills make it harder to balance books), and the sense of layout. **(2)** Animation keys. For **DaDA**, an Amiga computer system was used: a simple video downshooter; a digitizer; and Take Two line-test software, so the animation could be tested and refined throughout. 'It helps to be able to evaluate your work in progress. I animated my very first no-budget film **The Balencer** "blind". After I had finished the entire film I shot a 16mm pencil test. A very sobering experience. There was no way to alter things.' **(3-6)** Stills from **DaDA**: note the 'happy', 'innocent' cartoon look.

(7-8) T.R.A.N.S.I.T: Development art by Pieter Hoogenbirk.

7   8

1

2

3

4

5

6

(1–15) **T.R.A.N.S.I.T**: 'A bored socialite lifts a butcher from his dreary existence, has a fling with him, then can't get rid of him. He follows her across continents and she winds up chopped into bits in her own suitcase.' Kroon looked for a different graphic style to suit each sequence. (1) Venice sequence animated by Keiko Masuda; (2) still from SS L'Amérique du Sud, animated by Michaël Dudok de Wit and An Vrombaut. This sequence was inspired by Casandre's poster art; (3) St Tropez sequence by Valerie Carmona. (4) 'Some styles were set from the start, for example, late 19th-century Dutch social-realist poster style for the Amsterdam sequence by Arjan Wilschut, to reflect the butcher's working class background. The strongest colour is red and the linework is black and heavy, like in linoprints. The butcher is seduced by the colour and refinement of the upper class.' (5–9) Luggage label art developed by art director Gill Bradley, who comments: 'Good art direction is like good editing; it should be invisible. The story is always paramount, and all the backgrounds, colours and styles are there to enhance it. Look at the action, then complement and frame it if you want to focus on a particular element.'

7

8

9

10

11

12

(10–12) Given the geographic distance between the various animators, Bradley organised a video shoot, with professional actors, to provide reference material to ensure the continuity of each character's movements and gestures. This was particularly important given the film's stylistic diversity. The video shoot was used as a starting point for the character design and models. It was not used for rotoscoping. (13–15) Extracts from a discussion of Emmy's character conducted by fax between Kroon and Bradley.

I like the idea of the follow through action on the hair. Storywise however the look on her face at this point is extremely important! She's annoyed at FELIX, her boredom with him should come through, annoyed because she does not like being HONKED at. This look is where she resolves to go ahead and try and start an affair with OSCAR. (so she doesn't get the calling card out until after)

13

PIET!

HERE IS A MORE WOOD BLOCK STYLE EMMY — I THINK, ACTUALLY, SHE SHOULD HAVE MORE ELEGANT SWEEPING BRUSHSTROKE LINES — MORE LIKE THE OTHERS HERE — TO MAKE THE CONTRAST WITH OSCARS BLOCKY/ROUGH STYLE.

GILL.

EXPECT 2× DRAWINGS (A) → (E)

14

I'VE SLIGHTLY CHANGED THE STYLE OF DRESS COAT FOR EMMY (ie CUFFS) AND REMOVED THE SPOTS ON THE DRESS — AS A CONCESSION TO THE ANIMATORS! I DO HOWEVER, LIKE THE 'ERMINE' COAT.

EMMY + FELIX HAVE ELONGATED FEET/HANDS AND NECKS — UNLIKE OSCARS BLOCK STYLE.

EMMY AMSTERDAM

15

1

2

(1–9) **T.R.A.N.S.I.T**: Developing character models. *(1–2, 5–6)* Kroon's character designs to fit the highly stylised feel of the travel poster art that the L'Amerique du Sud sequence was based on. *(3–4)* Notes on the butcher's stylisation for the Amsterdam sequence. *(7–9)* The director's notes on elegant character posing.

3

4

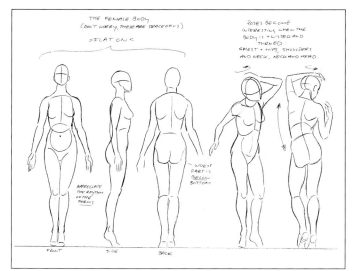

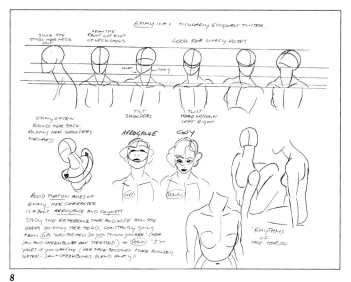

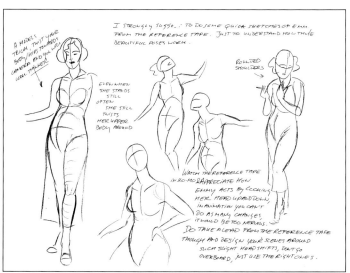

Kroon also uses the 'mirror and contrast' principle, which applies to all visual communication – and is therefore especially suited to wordless storytelling. 'The human mind is designed to organise and to apply structure, recognising patterns and similarities. Our eyes are drawn to exceptions. Looking for elements in the idea that mirror or contrast existing components can trigger more lists and improvements. Contrast drives the story forward. Closure is similarity, symmetry and a happy-ever-after; narrative is contrast, the glitch you want to see smoothed out.'

In 'dream' mode, Kroon wondered, 'What if a couple had a child that couldn't balance any books on its head?' which triggered most of the story. 'You roll with it, then go back and analyse it. Pull it into focus. It would be a bigger problem if the parents really wanted a smart child. More contrast if the father initially doesn't want a child, but his wife does. The little reptile in the fish tank represents the father's pride and joy. The newborn child takes its place (exemplifying the mirror principle) and is put on the same pedestal. When the child does not deliver, it's replaced by the pet again. And so on.'

T.R.A.N.S.I.T was prompted by a storyboard competition for a film about a suitcase. It was a small step from suitcase to art deco luggage labels – so evocative of the 1920s upperclass

lifestyle. As he explained the idea of telling the suitcase owner's story by retracing its travels, to his co-producer (and wife) Cecile Wijne, the story itself 'was dreamt up in a few minutes'.

Kroon feels it is important however, not to let 'dreamt up' sequences become rigid ideas, however powerful and illogically binding. 'You must try and reason with your stubborn dream-children, because often their real reason for being no longer applies. Story elements can be tied to ideas you decided to discard long ago. Force yourself to think again. With **T.R.A.N.S.I.T**, I finally replaced the original first half of the Orient Express sequence midway through making the film.'

His goal is not so much to tell a story, or to transfer content. Rather, he enjoys the process of storytelling. 'To manipulate the communication, to mess with people's minds. For the duration of your film you can lead the audience on, build their expectations, then turn the tables.' **DaDA** is a mild expression of this idea. The cartoon-like style and pastel colours suggest an innocent story; and its style of layout suggests a happy ending; but when the end comes, it is quite wry and dark.

T.R.A.N.S.I.T has a bolder narrative strategy in that the story is told backwards in time, it challenges the audience to figure out the non-chronological time-line and then fill in what has

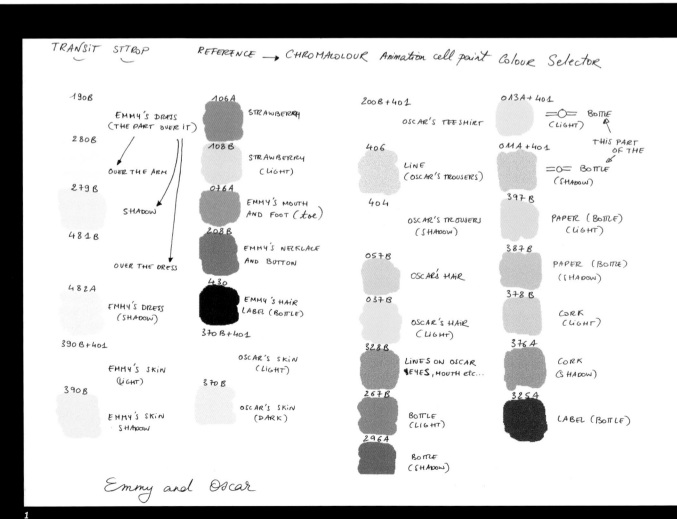

occurred between the sequences. This, combined with the disorienting change of graphic styles, adds up to a film that almost purposefully frustrates communication. While making the film Kroon was inclined at times to abandon this rigid formal concept and make the narrative chronological, but in the end he's happy he stuck to his guns. 'I want to make films that stay in people's minds and **T.R.A.N.S.I.T** invites you to think about it after it's over, to put the pieces of the puzzle together', he comments, adding, '**DaDA** would have been an inconsequential film if it had had a happy ending. By frustrating the desire for closure a short grows on people.'

Storyboards are, for him, 'the only way to get a grip on the story to see if it works as a film without dialogue. It's very easy to hide behind words. It's something else to tell the same story visually. Timing out the boards and creating the animatic changes your perception of the story: scenes that seemed to work like a charm on the boards are boring, or you realise they can be cut no matter how crucial they seemed.'

T.R.A.N.S.I.T's core concept was 'to use different graphic styles to give the element of style or design dramatic meaning' as Kroon describes it. A sense of his own limitations in terms of personal artistry, and the desire to make the film more quickly with a larger team, led him to think of casting different animators for the different segments. Initially he intended the film to be a type of ani-Jam project, with individual animators and animation directors working fairly autonomously. 'As long as they were telling the same story, they could feel free to alter the layouts, and shots, etc., but it turned out completely differently. I heavily directed every aspect of the picture, laid out all the scenes myself, in some cases providing rough animation keys and so forth.'

This was complicated by his being based in Los Angeles by the time UK producer Iain Harvey had raised the final budget. So he directed at long distance, faxing and e-mailing the animators who were working in different countries as drawings, layouts and animated sequences were sent back and forth. 'Iain Harvey did a tremendous producing job', says Kroon. 'Most producers would pass on such a complex, geographically challenged production. To a large degree, it's Iain's belief in the project and perseverance that made **T.R.A.N.S.I.T** the film it is. He's one of the most passionate producers I know.'

(1–2) **T.R.A.N.S.I.T**: Gill Bradley's colour instructions.

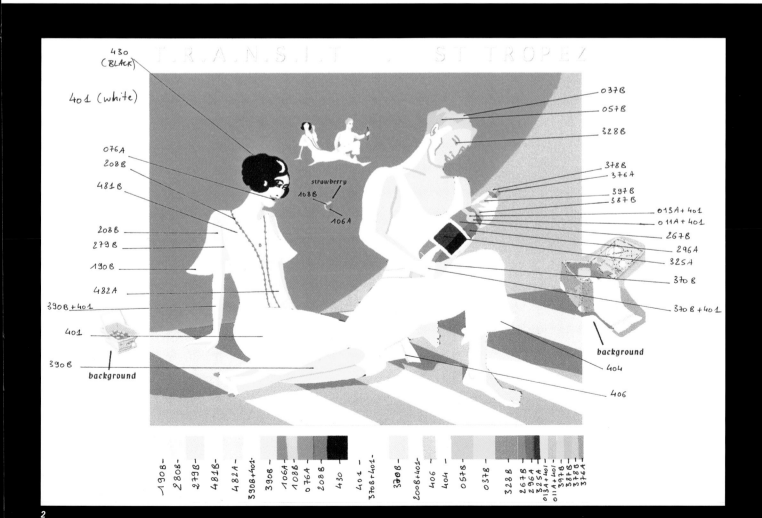

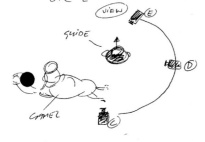

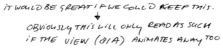

81C–E WAS ENVISIONED AS AN ANIMATED CAMERA MOVE

IT WOULD BE GREAT IF WE COULD KEEP THIS.

OBVIOUSLY THIS WILL ONLY READ AS SUCH
IF THE VIEW (81A) ANIMATES AWAY TOO

IF IT PROVES TOO COMPLEX, THERE IS AN
EASY WAY OUT: 81A + 81B – CUT – 81E
(WITH CAMEL CLOSER TO DRIVER, PAN UP
TO 82A → FOR 83 WE COULD THEN
PULL OUT TO A SHOT LIKE 81E.

1

2

Xeroxing pages from art deco books and grouping them per sequence, with notes, Kroon had compiled a style guide to kick off the art direction. When Gill Bradley came on board as art director, a role all the more crucial in this context, she did a great deal of research and experimentation to get the styles they wanted to work for animation, playing to the strengths of the individual talents concerned, whilst ensuring each segment worked within the film as a whole. 'Production manager Ian McCue also helped develop the techniques, in particular for the Orient Express sequence. This came out very differently from what I'd imagined and it looked much better. All of that is Gill and Ian's combined brilliance.'

5

6

(1–6) **T.R.A.N.S.I.T**: *(1)* Kroon's instructions to Andrew Higgins for a scene in the Egypt sequence. *(3)* Still from the final scene. *(3–4)* Stills from the Orient Express sequence that was animated by Jeroen van Blaaderen. *(4–6)* For the Orient Express sequence, several kinds of glue *(6)* were tested to achieve the glass relief effect of René Lalique's 'Bacchanalian Maidens' that inspired the design of the sequence. The final look was arrived at by painting a resist fluid onto cel in the same way as traditional cel-painting. Once dried the fluid gave a flat, frosted effect. The film was shot on different passes using blue gels and light fog filters on an airbrushed background. A white trace line on the cel was overlaid as the final layer.

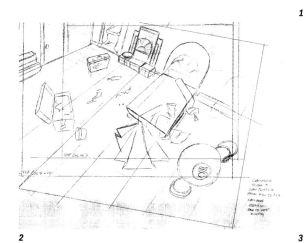

1

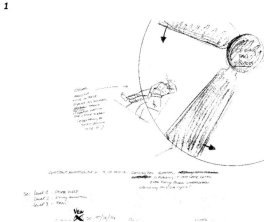

(1–8) **T.R.A.N.S.I.T.** *(1–4)* Layout sketches for the bedroom scene in the Venice sequence. *(5–6)* Stills from Nicolette van Gendt's Baden sequence. *(7–8)* Extracts from Kroon's bulging folders of faxes and e-mails, usually several pages long, sent variously to animators, the art director, and the editor.

2

3

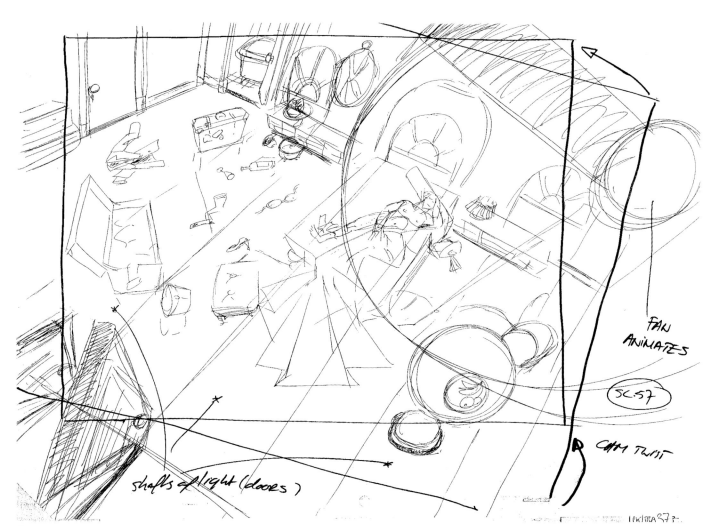

FAN ANIMATES

SC 57

CAM TWIST

shafts of light (doors)

4

5

6

7

(1–4) **The Three Inventors:**
As there was no focus viewer,
the balloon and the white bird's
superimposition required
several takes.

(5–7) **Princes et Princesses:**
In an abandoned cinema, a boy
and girl, using encyclopaedias
and computer technology as a
springboard, invent stories which
they act out.

The film has in fact sold to 34 countries, from the USA (despite the much quoted Anglo-Saxon prudery) to China, and in Norway **Kirikou** has become a national favourite. Ocelot feels this is because 'it's a story from the heart and people respond to that'. The film's global success has disproved predictions of limited cultural reach: 'Japanese journalists told me the cultural translations they usually have to make to understand Western films weren't necessary with **Kirikou**!' The film was also enthusiastically received in Africa.

Another factor in the film's success is repeat admissions: just as small children often demand the same story is read to them over and over, so they seem to respond to the film. The audience age range has surprised Ocelot himself. 'Although I knew that children are not stupid... when writing, I had in mind children who'd attained the age of reason, around seven years old, as the story was quite involved. Then I saw cinemas full of five-year-olds, completely transfixed – no fidgeting or talking.' The film also worked for kids as young as two and three. 'As a child, you don't understand absolutely everything around you, that's life, and it's the same with a film. What they don't understand they can guess and it doesn't bother them. But they know I am taking them seriously, not talking down to them, and that what I say is true. They feel it – in the way we distinguish between a fake foreign language an actor invents and a foreign language we've never heard before.' One child complained about Kirikou's running so fast, 'because otherwise the film would've lasted longer' but perhaps the highest accolade came from another who said: 'That's the best Disney I've ever seen!'

1

2

3

4

5

7

(1-7) Princes et Princesses:
(1, 5-7) Ocelot's love of Egyptian art, and Japanese refinement inspired two of the six episodes. The characters were cut out of black drawing paper in two sizes, one for long-shot and another for close-up, and articulated with wire. **(3)** Some details however, were made on cel, for example the princess' lace trim. Animation was done under-camera. **(1)** Layers of thin glass allowed tracing paper to be used for mist, or laid over a rough watercolour to transform it into a soft sky, or for Japanese screens. **(2)** When the animation was more simple, other techniques were used, including plasticine for the slug, salt for foam, cotton wool for clouds, and sometimes regular cel animation for character transformations.

For **The Three Inventors**, Ocelot adapted a cut-out technique invented by the animator J-F Laguionie – an imaginative mis-use of office stationery to stick and move thin metallised card on a magnetic sheet, like fridge magnets in reverse. Laguionie's cut-outs left no shadow, but had to be moved as whole elements; whereas Ocelot wanted a bas-relief effect, and to move particular parts of his characters. He articulated them with scraps of the 'metallic' card so even the smallest gesture could be easily and precisely controlled. **(5)** Ocelot's research is meticulous: viz the accuracy of his 18th dynasty Egyptian queen's headress. 'It's part of the hidden harmony: every note has to ring true – even if the audience is unaware, it works better.' **(6)** A way to show the day passing. **(7)** The horn and tree shapes come from Egyptian tomb paintings.

European Union co-production rules required three countries to invest, with part of the work being done in each – in **Kirikou**'s case, Paris and Angouleme in France, Luxembourg and Brussels. To keep costs down, animation was done in Latvia and Hungary, and the voices and Youssou N'Dour's score were recorded in Senegal. This meant four years' gruelling travel between the dispersed sites, and posed obvious co-ordination problems. In future, Ocelot would prefer things 'on a more human scale: myself and the whole team working together in one place'.

Ocelot considers the storyboard to be the true authorial imprint and he only writes the definitive dialogue once it's finished. 'It's only then that you can see something is missing, or is redundant because the image says it all.' When adding sound, he won't work with a guide track, preferring the animators to work with the edited recording, songs and music for dances. 'Playing with sound in all its aspects is an integral part of the filmmaking process.'

A self-taught animator, he feels he was preparing for this vocation from early childhood. The family had no TV, and didn't often go to the cinema, so he created his own entertainment, drawing and dressing up, and making things from bric-a-brac. A defining moment in his teens was discovering a Pollock-style cut-out puppet theatre. The half-fake sense of volume appealed, and soon he was creating his own. Animated films followed when he found a do-it-yourself manual on stop-frame motion.

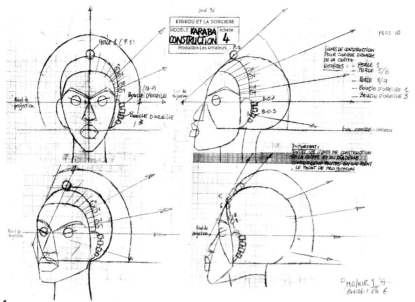

1

4

2

5

6

3

7

(1–11) **Kirikou**: Character designs and stills. (8–11) The fetish figures have been interpreted as robots, an inappropriate concession to the youth market, but were actually the film's most African elements, modelled on sculpture styles from Guinea, Nigeria, the Congo and the Gabon. (12) A cartoon depicting Ocelot's ceaseless travel for this co-production, and his actual mode of transportation when in Paris.

12

KIRIKOU EN VOYAGE

8

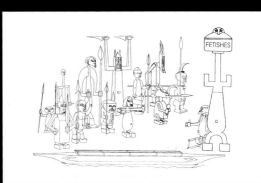

10

9

11

1

5

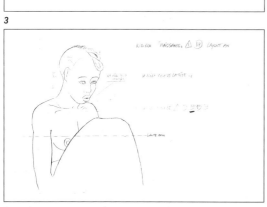

2

3

6

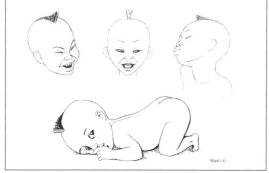

4

7

8

(1–11) Kirikou: Ocelot's first feature film. The fairly conventional graphic style was designed to reassure producers and investors. After working with black, graphic silhouettes on **Princes et Princesses,** Ocelot found that he initially felt 'ashamed of becoming so ordinary, vulgar and "cartoon-like"', but then realised, 'I'd forgotten how interesting full colour was'.

(9–10) Ocelot's childhood memories fed into the background design, but as there is no graphic tradition in African art, which tends more to sculpture and architecture, he decided to aim for a 'black Douanier Rousseau' effect. Background artists drew and painted each element separately – and they were then replicated and put together using computers. Changing colour values and hues at will on computer was like 'a return to the intense painterly pleasures of art school – but easier, given the speed at which one can make changes and keep all versions.'

9

10

'**Filmmaking** is like a continuation of childhood play. Apart from the important "bricolage" aspect of animation, there's a moral dimension to playing with magic tricks: don't believe all you're told, or all you see; it's not a miracle, there's always an explanation.' He likes the obvious artifice of silhouettes and cut-outs, the complicity with an audience it can create, saying of the displays: 'It's obvious this is a story we are going to play together, and believe in'.

Whilst studying painting, engraving and sculpture, Ocelot also did a little theatre, classical and modern dance. A well-thumbed library of art books testifies to his love of looking at pictures. Egyptian and Greek art were his earliest influences, and later, English and French 19th-century illustration, Japanese art – particularly Hokusai, Italian Renaissance, symbolism, '20s and '30s figurative artists and contemporaries such as Moebius – 'Pictures that tell stories and contain good drawing'.

Ocelot resents the time animation takes. For **Kirikou**: 'Two years to raise the money, and four years to make something written in a week. Every new film teaches us something and if I could make ten films instead of one I'd learn ten times as much.' He hopes computers might eventually help speed the process up. 'I have more projects and desires than I will be able to achieve in my lifetime.'

11

Priit Pärn

Engineering narrative

1

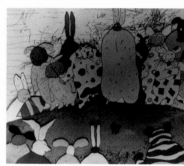

2

Estonian filmmaker Priit Pärn credits an element of his highly distinctive approach to animation to his scientific training. Whilst working as an environmental scientist, he established a reputation for his satirical, politically edgy cartoons and caricatures; he also produced several children's books before he came to animation in his early 30s. His films are visually highly inventive and often explore complex ideas. He divides his films into those made after the Soviet period, and those made before. Production on the latter had to be authorised by the official censors – although he often 'cheated' to circumvent this. His narratives, however unconventional, are always quite analytically developed, and have generated many a graduate thesis.

His development of ideas in his early shorts varied from film to film. Rather than storyboard **And Now Play Tricks**, he marked off sheets of ruled paper into millimetres, each representing one second. He wrote an action against each second and then went direct to layout. He wrote the story for **Triangle**, a witty dissection of a dysfunctional relationship, on a single sheet of paper, then storyboarded with only minimal changes. For **Exercises for Independent Life**, he had the whole story already in his mind, so worked on construction and rhythm by writing each action – for example, opening a newspaper or picking a flower – on a slip of paper, then he played with the slips like a pack of cards to structure the film.

Pärn often tells his latest film's story to people, not for feedback but as he describes, 'to control the telling of the story, which at this stage might be written or still just ideas in my mind. If I can tell it, then it's probably ready and I can begin to storyboard.' If not, he knows further work is required. 'Whether I'm working on script, storyboard or layout, I have a range of techniques to take the ideas out of my head and find a construction for them.' Pärn is known for the exercises he sets his students; 'I teach them how to free your fantasy, how to organise this activity in your head. It's a combination of fantasy with the approach of an engineer or mathematician.'

Pärn's drawings set the graphic style and character design for his films, but the colours are developed by Miljard Kilk. Having worked together since 1982, Pärn finds, 'it is easy to explain my imagination to him. It's important that the colour doesn't kill the graphic line. I've always a basic idea of the role colour plays, but I don't say, "it must be grey here, yellow there". Miljard might do something and I'll say no, that's not what I mean. The next day I realise I couldn't come up with something better. The combination of colour and graphic design is so important that you have to really explore all possibilities before starting upon production.'

'Storyboarding means finding an audio visual form for the written story, so you have to think about sound at this stage. You can convey a lot of information in one sentence, but for the storyboard I have to decide whether information should be visual or audio, not just the voiceover aspect, but the whole soundtrack. If I can do something with sound rather than animate, it's cheaper, quicker and it can also be more exciting. Animation is a created world, with a much greater potential for combinations of sound and images than live-action.'

3

4

5

(1–6) Stills from early short films: *(1–2)* **And Now Play Tricks**; *(3–4)* **Time Out** and *(5–6)* **Triangle**.

6

1

2

3

4

5

(1–5) Stills and sketches for **Breakfast on the Grass**: (5) Estonian animator Mati Kütt, who worked on and featured briefly in the film. Pärn dislikes the classical Disney convention of using a different style background to that of the action, feeling that the same techniques should be used for both of them.

(6–10) **Hotel E**: (6) Storyboard extract; (7–10) stills and a preparatory sketch from the two short prologues – one using charcoal and cut-out, the other using oil paint – were intended to provide a key to the film. They suggested the model of a society with strict rules, and closed circles, which is disrupted by a breaking of the circle, and moving beyond the rules. These actions are repeated in different contexts throughout the rest of the film.

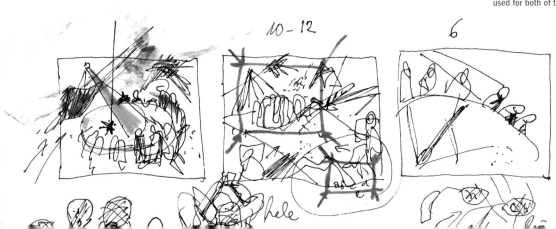

6

7

8

9

10

'In production you have to work like an animal. You can't stop. When you get so tired you fall off your chair you simply have to climb back on. The animation has to look like my drawings, but I have to simplify them for the optimum effect. And this optimum is quite close to a minimum.' For Pärn, checking all the drawings is the busiest and most boring phase: 'You lose all sense of day and night, and the process works like a huge machine. Once the animation is done and gone to trace and paint, it's a comparatively easy period, but when editing you have to be sharp, so you can't do 18 hours a day.'

After this long and tiring process, sound is, for Pärn: 'The first moment you feel someone else can do something for the film, since in the animation stage the surprises are usually negative.' He talks to his composer very early on, and gives him quite a free rein, although he's more directive on specific sound effects.

Pärn likes to animate a five to ten second sequence himself on each film – 'just for fun' – although he adds, 'I'm not fanatical about it, it's not my profession. I'm lucky I have others to do it.' As a filmmaker rather than an animator, he feels that often those with a purely animation background tend to focus overly on movement, rather than 'what is moving or why'.

Given the compression of animation, Pärn points out: 'In a 30-minute film – like the last four I've made – there's as much action as in a 90-minute live-action feature, therefore the scripting is quite different, it takes much longer.' Although he starts drawing as he writes, he finds that, 'the drawings aren't as important as for shorts such as **Triangle** or **Time Out** where visual tricks are played and gags developed'.

1

2

His first long film, **Breakfast on the Grass**, was an exploration of the difficulties of everyday life under the Soviet regime and a plea for artistic freedom. It took four years to pass the censor's office. This, and **Hotel E**, which contrasts life in the East and West and was made just after Estonia won independence from the Soviet Union, had an enormous impact and made his international reputation. His next film, **1895**, was a radical departure in its introduction of voiceover narration, as all his previous films had been wordless. Commissioned as a film for the centenary of the invention of the cinema, it is a complex, serious *and* irreverent discourse on history, culture and the individual. The narration plays off and sometimes against the images rather than explicating them, in a manner many have compared to the later work of French filmmaker Jean-Luc Godard. Pärn does not see why he should be restricted to Western expectations based on his previous films, which some have taken more seriously because they can be read, somewhat reductively, as political parables. 'If I'm only fighting against something, I'm imprisoned by my enemy. If it's a dramatic narrative – I am a prisoner of my story. I want the freedom to have fun. Now the Soviet regime is over, I can be more frivolous.'

3

(1–8) Hotel E: (1–3) The dark scenes, representing the East, used several cel layers under the camera to build up the shadows. Several hours were spent getting it right for two to three seconds of screen time. **(4–8)** The West, seen as rich yet vacuous, is in colour. The animation was rotoscoped, which underscores the repetitiveness of the life portrayed. Interiors were drawn on cel, then partly painted by Miljard with normal cel paint on special paper; the textured 'Jackson Pollock' effects were made as prints, then cut out and laid under cel. A palette of only 14 colours was used, and to create an impression of more, three months were spent balancing the colour. The work carried out on colour design took a total of five months.

4

8

He continues, 'When you make films without words you have to spend so much time moving the story along. It's not true that animation has no limits. Without words you have to keep it simpler, which limits what you can do. It's more like creating slogans. How else can you visually convey and be understood?' With **1895**, the main idea was this: from what you see on screen and what you hear, something else emerges. As human beings we are endowed with language, so why should I be afraid to use it? It's impossible to make complicated stories without words. I like to work with different levels of meaning, to have an open system, unlike short films that just take you to the ending. Some things might mean something only to Estonians, others to anyone who's lived under a particular political system, and of course mostly the films contain a lot that can be understood by anyone at all.'

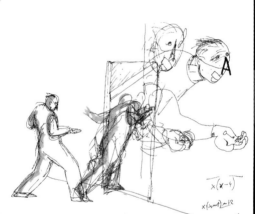

1

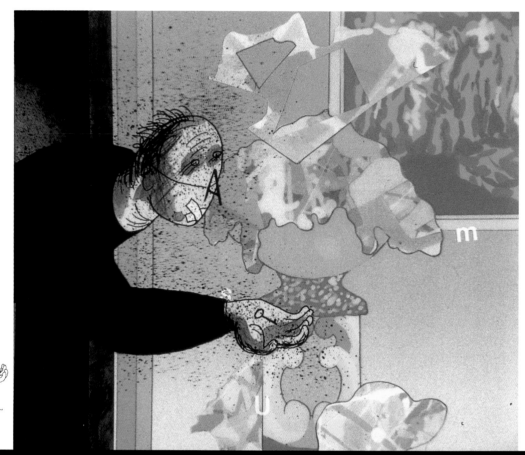

2

3

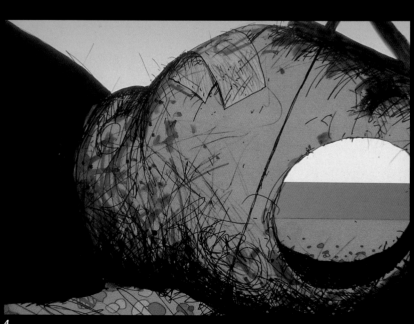

4

(1–5) **Hotel E**: Sketch and stills. *(6–8)* **1895** is ostensibly a film about the centenary of the cinema. For Pärn, research is somewhat irrelevant, since 'animation is a fantasy world'. However, for **1895**, he did check Lumière's birthdate to ensure against using the correct one by mistake, as all the dates cited in the film are fictitious. A photograph of Lumière smoking prompted a running motif in what the director calls his 'pseudo-French film'.

As a budding caricaturist, he had 'idols' among his peers, but, apart from seeing some Polish animation in the '70s which aroused his interest in the medium's potential as an art form, Pärn feels that by the time he came to make animation films he was quite developed as a person and an artist. If anything, live-action was a stronger influence, and he admires the work of Federico Fellini and Peter Greenaway. 'I don't particularly like watching animation, and I find a lot of it boring', he comments, although he does admit to liking the films of the Quay Brothers.

In terms of having an audience in mind, Pärn feels that 'the only honest way to make film is if you are free in your imagination, and the only measurement of that is yourself. Each new film is quite different. Actually my only motivation – the reason I continue – is the element of risk, I make the film to find out if the construction in my head will work, to see it.'

Unlike the Western tradition of auteur animation, where filmmakers often work by themselves or with minimal crews, Soviet animation was organised on the studio system, with large teams and a division of labour. Post-Perestroika, state funding has diminished dramatically, and although in Estonia his work has continued to be financially supported, Pärn is aware that the new market economy might make things difficult in the future. 'Until now, we've still been able to make our films with small budgets because the standard of living is low, so we could afford to have a lot of people working on a non-commercial film. I couldn't do it by myself: it's expensive and takes too long, I need to make my films quickly.' He is rather pessimistic about the current directions animation is taking: 'Films have either to be long and boring or kitschy and clever stories which say nothing. However, I have to say that I have been lucky in being able to do what I want.'

As far as his own work is concerned, he is currently developing a live-action feature film, and continues to work as an artist. 'It's been 13 years since the changes in 1988. We've been quite free, and we have some experiences that the West hasn't had. Even in the Soviet period, we knew more about the West than the West knew about us. Now the differences are larger. Our generation is unprecedented. The question is how to use this and why?'

1

2

Diego

4

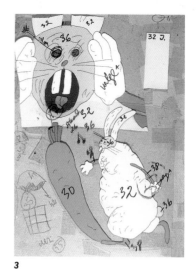

5

3

6

Diego the lonely cyclist, the adorer of everything round, the hater of everything angular, the man who had everything written right in his face

then Diego saw Steffi, no angles, just round. Steffi was a hard boiled egg

Michael was a stripeless zebra who ...dreamed of marrying the fattest woman in the world, as soon as that woman had been found, and as soon as he himself was ready for it.

Mikhail....dreamed of rounding up all the people in the world and making them happy. He was prevented from doing this by a strange force which pulled him up to the ceiling.

.....The great cellist sees in his dreams the solution to Mikhail's mystery. Helmut's room is situated exactly above his room. Helmut's bottom has a plus charge and Mikhail's head has a minus charge. Helmut falling on his bottom causes Mikhail to be pulled up to the ceiling.
Mikhail never learned it was Helmut's falling in the recent past which had destroyed his life. The present for Mikhail contained only the knowledge that he didn't want to go back and he couldn't go forward.

The very moment the rabbits knew how to combine electronic hi-tech and voodoo, their position in starting and controlling the global processes was beyond competition. The range of their ever expanding rabbit interests included just about eveyything. Initially small producers of ketchup, the rabbits had grown to be a leading super power of the world, but their hearts still belonged to ketchup.
The rabbits considered themselves a global force, they believed they were everwhere like the Holy Ghost. In reality the rabbits inhabited the upper floors of PGI. Everyone knew this except for the rabbits themselves.

7

8

9

(1-11) The Night of the Carrots:
(1-6) Character designs with
colour number instructions;
(7) extracts from the voiceover
narration; (8-9, 11) storyboard
sketches. When Pärn starts
storyboarding he's still
developing the graphic style, and
tends to work simultaneously on
layout. 'The small storyboard
sketches are just for me and the
colour artist - for composition;
whereas the larger, i.e. normal,
artwork size of 12 fields is for
work on developing the
characters, with more space for
small details in action and story.
The boards are marked up for
basic composition and camera
movements and are quite rough,
but this is enough for the
animators to understand.'
(10) Still.

10

11

12

(12-14) Pärn's work as an artist:
Etchings and charcoal drawings.
'There are a lot of ideas which
might later be usable in a film.
Sometimes when working with a
script I find a visual solution in
my drawings.'

13   14

Daniel Greaves

Exploring different techniques

Although every one of Daniel Greaves' animated films looks completely different, they are all driven by the same impetus: a celebration of the formal potential of animation itself.

'I was into magic tricks as a kid – seeing people react to what is essentially a trick of the eye is always exciting and fun to watch – and that's what animation is really about. At 13 I started experimenting with animation, fascinated by the process as much as the result. I found I could draw better than I could perform tricks! It's like inventing your own magic trick and adding it to a box of already established ones.'

Certain themes recur in Greaves' films, especially metamorphosis, and reality versus fantasy. For him, these themes are unconsciously woven in as a visual idea sparks off a stream of subconscious thoughts – thus the film's shape evolves quite freely. Some ideas are heavily edited and some re-surface several years later, if he finds they still have appeal. 'I've always got a bank of ideas in my head and notebooks of scribbled jottings and sketches. Anything, even a flawed idea, is worth noting. You never know.'

The technique usually comes first as Greaves finds inspiration in the 'look' of the film and experiments to develop the technique before embarking on a storyline. 'I'm eager to start animating, as I like the natural changes that take place during this process.' Even when satisfied with a tight and detailed storyboard, Greaves does not expect to adhere to every panel, as new ideas emerge, changing the narrative for the better. Tighter storyboards are more important with commercials, which have a very specific brief and duration.

'When animating, although I roughly plan out a scene, I'm often disappointed with the first line test. But I seem to need to go through this painful process, as I instinctively know how to correct the action and approach the scene in an entirely different way. It's an alarming amount of time and effort expended, but it helps to perfect the action: a classic example of learning directly from your mistakes.

1

2

(1–2) Early sketches and pencil drawings for **Manipulation**. 'The film came about through a fortuitous accident: reviewing a line test, I froze the image on a frame where I'd accidentally passed my hand in front of the camera. It looked as though the hand was reacting with the character on paper: an idea I thought I could develop, starting with the animator's desk in a studio, then closing in on a sheet of paper and a hand drawing of a character, which is then scrapped (another autobiographical reference!). However, the character returns, refusing to be beaten, so battle ensues between the creator and his creation.'

(3–4) Stills from **Manipulation**. 'The story evolved organically – it really didn't need a strong narrative, being more of a performance. I'd rough out a very quick animation, test the drawings for timing, and make adjustments to improve the drawings which were then re-shot with my hands in place manipulating the character. 'I kept going until I'd exhausted ideas on the theme. I concocted several alternative endings, but finally opted for the character, in a final desperate attempt, emerging from the paper in 3D, before finally ending up as a flat image again. **Flatworld** here we come!'

3

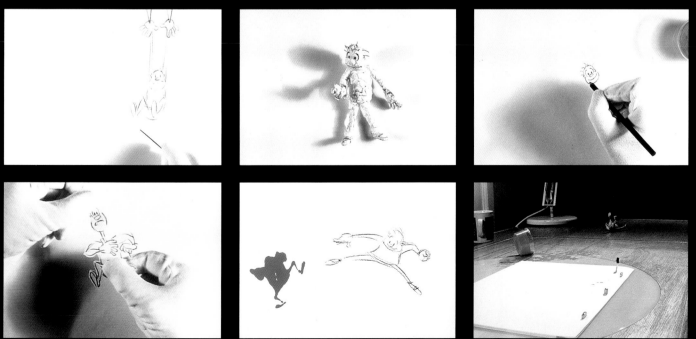

4

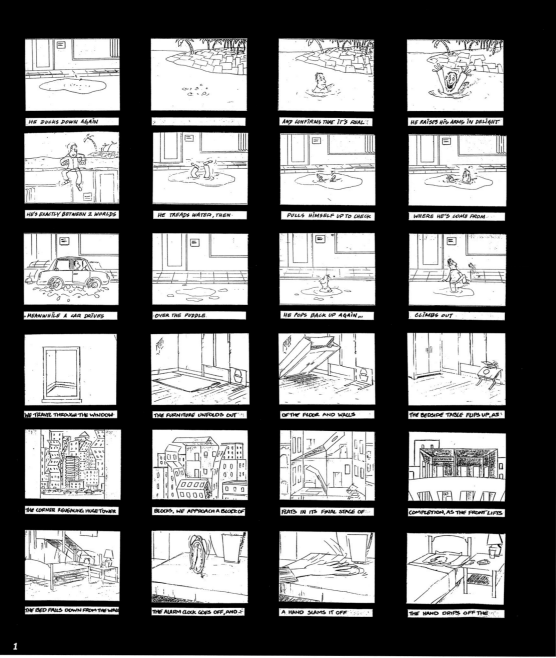

HE DUCKS DOWN AGAIN

AND CONFIRMS THAT IT'S REAL.

HE RAISES HIS ARMS IN DELIGHT

HE'S EXACTLY BETWEEN 2 WORLDS

HE TREADS WATER, THEN

PULLS HIMSELF UP TO CHECK

WHERE HE'S COME FROM

·MEANWHILE A CAR DRIVES·

·OVER THE PUDDLE·

HE POPS BACK UP AGAIN...

CLIMBS OUT

WE TRAVEL THROUGH THE WINDOW·

THE FURNITURE UNFOLDS OUT

OF THE FLOOR AND WALLS

THE BEDSIDE TABLE FLIPS UP, AS·

THE CORNER REVEALING HUGE TOWER

BLOCKS, WE APPROACH A BLOCK OF

FLATS IN ITS FINAL STAGE OF

COMPLETION, AS THE FRONT LIFTS

THE BED FALLS DOWN FROM THE WALL·

THE ALARM CLOCK GOES OFF, AND·

A HAND SLAMS IT OFF

THE HAND DRIPS OFF THE

1

TV WORLDS

① WESTERN
② QUIZ SHOW (STUDIO INTERIOR)
③ SCI-FI
④ SPORTS - FOOTBALL, TENNIS, HORSE RACING, GOLF, SNOOKER, RUGBY etc.
⑤ NEWSREADER / WEATHERMAN (INTERIOR)
⑥ CHILDRENS PROGRAMMES
⑦ OPEN UNIVERSITY
⑧ SOAP OPERA
⑨ DOCUMENTARY
⑩ NATURE/WILDLIFE
⑪ HOLIDAY PROGRAMME

There should be equal emphasis on both sides. Also a scene involving a split screen effect where maybe Matt is pulling his cat through into Flat-world, and the fish is trying to pull it back into the Underworld

cut-out

Drawn

2

A man's hat is blown off

Everyone braces themselves

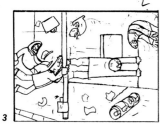

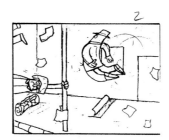

3

but are inevitably blown away by the fierce wind.

4

8

5

6

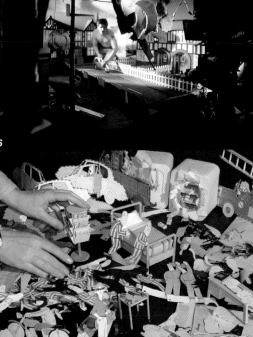

7

(1–8) **Flatworld**: *(1–2)* An extract from storyboards, and lists of ideas. *(3)* Storyboard for the sight gag 'Windy Street'. This was the first idea, where all the characters in an urban landscape get blown away by a violent wind. It was subsequently dropped from the film due to cost and time constraints. Grabbing at lampposts highlighted the nature of the characters being flat and cut out of paper, thus vulnerable to the elements. Greaves comments, 'although it's important for the story to carry the film along, it was fun to remind the audience of the cardboard cut-out sets and characters.' *(4–8)* Production stills. Each set, made entirely from card or paper, took around three months to create. Some model and propmakers preferred working on the larger-scale buildings. Others, with a watchmaker's mentality and patience, worked on tiny props.

Over 40,000 cut-outs were needed – each taking an hour to artwork: this involved them being drawn onto paper, photocopied, coloured, then mounted on stiff card and cut out with a scalpel, reinforced with lead weight and numbered sequentially. 12 sequential cut-out characters were used for 24 frames, i.e. one second. A core team of 40 people worked on the film, although around a hundred were involved overall.

'The most exhilarating aspect of filmmaking is the buzz of coming up with ideas. The hard part is translating faithfully these thoughts and images onto paper. All the stages of production are enjoyable, although each has its own problems along the way. Pre-production alternates between creative bursts of formulating and developing ideas and the inevitable practicalities of dealing with finance. Once in production, there are many rewards including the interaction of creative talents. Whatever medium you work in, inevitably there are moments when the process can become painfully tedious.'

'Post-production is enormously satisfying. Unless animating tightly to a track, for example on a commercial, sound is added afterwards. Sound is extremely important and it's a delight to witness the magic when the sound and images combine. Sound effects themselves can be very funny and enhance the visuals enormously. This stage always feels therapeutic – all the pressure and stress during production seems to fade away as the film comes alive. Russell Pay has collaborated with me on sound on all the films and several commercials. We prefer home-made sound effects, which feel more authentic, rather than effects from sound libraries, which sound slightly electronic.'

Manipulation, a short made over two and a half years in between commercials, won an Academy Award and brought Greaves to the attention of the BBC's Animation Unit, who suggested he make a half-hour TV special, which became the highly ambitious and technically innovative **Flatworld**.

Originating as a sketch of the world as a flat disc, and a number of sight gags involving 'flat jokes', the initial idea was to show how **Flatworld** came to be, formed from floating sheets of paper in a cosmos cluttered by a variety of office stationery. Greaves was concerned at the length and over-ambitiousness of this and, feeling that narrative was not his strong point, brought in Patrick Veale, a live-action writer for TV drama. Veale helped tighten up the storyboard, using his experience to craft an immediately gripping tale.

1

2

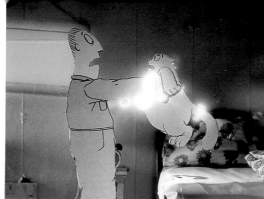

3

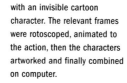

4

5

6

(1–8) Effects and animated characters were added digitally to **Flatworld** in post-production. The line test gave a good idea of roughly what the character was doing, but not knowing the size or location of the digital image can be difficult for the animator – rather like the set-up in the film **Who Framed Roger Rabbit**, where a real actor performs with an invisible cartoon character. The relevant frames were rotoscoped, animated to the action, then the characters artworked and finally combined on computer.

(7–8) Sketch and still of the main character's cat falling through a puddle in **Flatworld** into Flipside.

7

8

Rabbit Rabbit

6

2

4

1

3

5

(1–5) Stills from the sight gags in **Flatworld**: these were based on what could happen if flat cut-out characters were put into a 3D world.

(6) Rabbit Rabbit: The blue rabbit character, over a white background, multiplies to eventually fill the whole screen, then a white rabbit enters, over the blue background and the action repeats. The rabbit was animated to hop around the screen. This very simple action becomes a complex kaleidoscopic pattern for which the drawings were flipped over, traced off again, then folded, traced off, folded and so on.

1

2   *3*

Most of the film, at that point, led up to the protagonist, Matt, pushing his head through a puddle and discovering the Flipside of the world. Greaves then came up with the idea of the superhighway cable being severed, creating an aura which on contact with the puddles of water, transports Matt into Flipside – a channel-hopping cable TV world with a traditional drawn-cartoon look. Veale suggested Matt be falsely accused of robbery, as a great excuse for chase sequences throughout the film and a format for exploiting the humour of contrasting the two worlds.

The design was a collaboration between set designer Gordon Allen, lighting cameraman, Simon Paul and Greaves, who remembers, 'It had to look like it was all bolted together with staples and tape. Gordon had never done anything like this before, he just jumped in at the deep end and did some fantastic stuff. After a while, the model- and prop-makers really got into it, looking for anything made of paper or card they could use: office stationery catalogues suddenly came into their own!'

'I admire animators who understand and respect the materials they use, making a statement about the materiality, such as the oil paint in Clive Walley's work, or the tactility of the clay in Svankmajer's **Dimensions of Dialogue**. In **Flatworld** my chosen material was cardboard. I hoped the same effect would be achieved.'

4

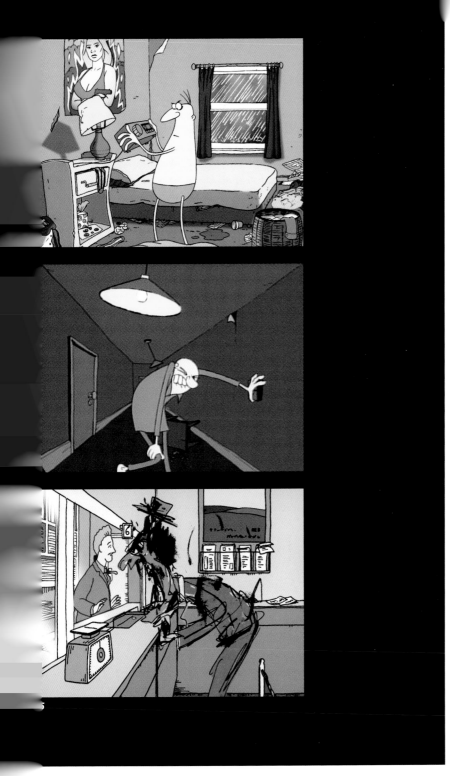

Greaves' fertile imagination can lead to frustration. 'I spend so much time developing ideas to quite an advanced state then abandoning them, out of boredom or insecurity, and then starting the whole process again. Even when I'm committed financially to a project, my mind wanders and I'm nagged by insecurities.' Worries about lack of time means Greaves thinks whilst committing pencil to paper, finding an urgency to physically capture the magic and energy of the original concept. This need to rush into a project feeds a prodigious productivity. **Flatworld**'s budget was almost twice the average for a TV special and so during the long period of fundraising, Greaves produced his own short, **Rabbit Rabbit**. 'Suddenly it dawned on me that I hadn't completed a film for four years! I had a notion of a character unwittingly duplicating himself through a variety of invisible trapdoors – a rabbit seemed appropriate for obvious reasons.

'After the epic **Flatworld** I needed to return to making very short succinct films. We're developing a series of short, punchy films, called **Little Things**. Each film features a range of differently designed characters, by different animators, with their own style of humour. Gradually, after several independent scenarios, the characters begin to invade each other's stories – rather like a jigsaw – interacting within the narrative. I don't like to get bogged down with one idea for too long, it becomes counter-productive. This particular project plays to my strengths, and the way my mind constantly jumps from one idea to another. I'm not quite sure how we're going to do it at the moment, but that's the challenge!'

If money were no object, Greaves would like to break away from character-based animation and investigate animation further in genre terms. 'I like atmospheres and creating moods. Humour is always going to be there – but I like the idea of creating terror and real suspense, out of animation, which is extremely difficult to do.' Enjoying the challenge of both 2D and 3D, Greaves also feels animation still has some way to go in combining them, and is currently working on an idea combining models and straight-drawn characters with a hidden twist.

1–4) 'With most commercials we get quite a free hand with the design, for example: *(1)* British Airways; *(2)* **Schweppes** and *(3)* **Tesco**; although some ads have been commissioned on the back of a film, such as *(4)* **Hellman's Mayonnaise** and *(6)* **Very Fine Apple Quenchers**.

(5) **Little Things**: Work in progress for Greaves' current project.

Koji Morimoto

A high tension approach

Koji Morimoto began his career in the animation industry after finishing art school, where he majored in animation, working for three years as art director on TV series such as **Ashita no Joe2**, **Space Cobra** and **Lensman**. Following this he went freelance. He was then invited to work as an animation supervisor on the cult cyberpunk movie **Akira**, the first Japanese animated feature to make a major impact in the West. Co-ordinating animation artwork and backgrounds to maintain the film's stylistic unity taught him how to assess the contributions that individual talents and skills could bring to a project. He recalls his two years there as intensely stimulating, with a fantastic work atmosphere created by the director, Katsuhiro Otomo. 'He had total charisma and it was such a joyous experience that I didn't want to leave', Morimoto remembers. Five years later, Otomo asked Morimoto to direct a segment of his portmanteau feature film, **Memories**.

Intensely involved with music, Morimoto has made several animated promos which pack highly complex narratives into a few short minutes. His promo for Japanese techno star Ken Ishii, **Extra**, brought him cult status on the club scene in both East and West. He is also one of the very few Japanese animators represented through a London-based studio, the award-winning Nexus Films, for whom he made the Bluetones promo 'Friday Weekend'. Nexus producer Chris O'Reilly comments, 'Seeing **Extra** – a film that seemed to have a different scale of ambition to other animation – revolutionised my attitude to the medium. If ever you need to refute the commonly held notions outside the industry that animation is either quirky and parochial, for kids or "artsy", look no further than his work. Slick, dark, sexy, dangerous but highly extrovert, his films are what James Cameron or Ridley Scott would make if they were animators. Animation needs people like Koji to push out the boundaries, to encompass new audiences. Japanese animation excellence has long been recognised in the West but there has still been woefully little co-production and collusion. It was a real privilege to work with a director whose work we all admired so strongly.'

Morimoto finds that: 'Visual ideas for a piece may arise from listening to music, or come to mind when drinking and chatting with people'. As he sketches, he's already got a clear picture of the final result he's after. He then discusses his ideas and appropriate techniques with his team. 'Although such discussion is useful, the disadvantage is that in the Japanese animation industry, production staff who join a project because of its director tend to be over-awed by their admiration, and high expectations can create pressure on the director, which is a heavy burden of responsibility.'

1

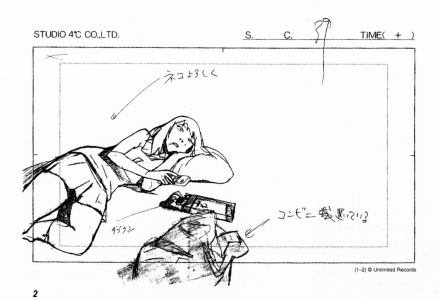

STUDIO 4℃ CO.,LTD.　　　　S.　　C.　　TIME(+)

ネコよろしく

コンビニ袋思い2113

クラフラ

(1–2) © Unlimited Records

2

8

(1–8) Drawings and stills from **Survival**: A promo for the popular Japanese group Glay. Unusually for him, Morimoto set the story in the present, featuring an ordinary teenage girl, so the audience could identify with it more easily.
(9) Poster for the short film **Noiseman Sound Insect**.

3

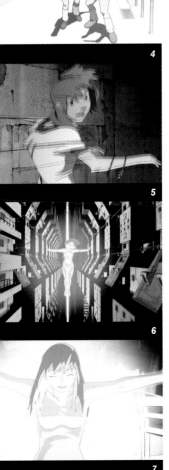

4

5

6

7

音響生命体

ノイズマン

（仮称）

'96/5/20

STUDIO 4℃

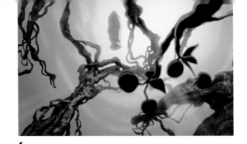

1

2

3

4

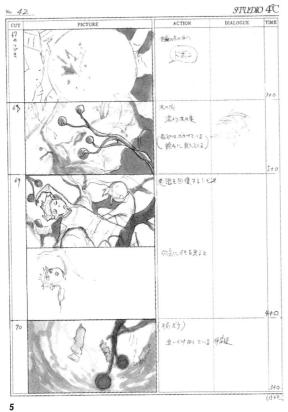

5

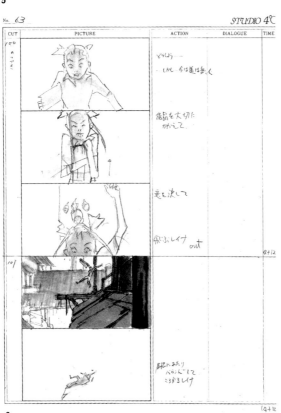

6

7

Design and visual style are decided first, and Morimoto works out each shot as he writes the script. 'Storyboards and scripts are very important. If the concepts and construction sketches are no good, it can all fall to pieces. Script, storyboard and music constitute 90 per cent of the work's impact.' He feels that traditional animation techniques are important because they provide an opportunity to do interesting things by breaking the rules: 'Without the tradition, such reversals lose effect'.

His first rough scenario goes through consultation with his team, then after it has been written up, he adds final personal touches. He creates storyboards, adding, 'there's not much to think about after that'. As he creates and designs both characters and backgrounds, by the time the storyboard is finished, he knows exactly how many drawings will be needed. Much of the remaining work is simply sitting and drawing. 'Whereas you can work on the concept for a scenario whilst having a sociable time, or taking a walk, being deskbound can be boring and stressful.' To alleviate this, he always tries to find new aspects to the work that will maintain his motivation. 'Anything unexpected in the production process is most welcome. It's what makes working with a variety of people interesting.'

Discussing his work, he uses the English word 'tension', which in Japanese means 'a good spirit'; a combination of energy, motivation and enthusiasm. If a project he's pitched for doesn't get accepted, he ascribes this to his lack of ability, and regrets his failure to maintain his tension in such cases. He also feels that, 'in the past, I sometimes tended to play to the audience, relying on stereotypes and clichés, and wasn't able to put my emotions into individual scenes'. This realisation of the importance of maintaining tension was perhaps a reason for going freelance. He now only accepts commissions if the project instinctively and immediately appeals and he can already see the film in his mind.

Working on **Memories** also taught him the importance of tension in relation to his team. When approached by staff with questions on something they had pondered for some time, he felt that it would be disrespectful if he did not maintain their tension. 'It was not that I felt bad for the staff, but rather I found that I couldn't respond to them sufficiently without bringing my own tension up.'

(1–8) Noiseman Sound Insect: A 25-minute film made for the DVD format, set in the distant future. A music-hating scientist creates a synthetic lifeform called Noiseman to erase music from the airwaves and fill the city with noise. A group of street biker kids fight back in a densely packed and frenetically paced narrative. **(1–4)** Sketches; **(5–7)** storyboard extracts; **(8)** stills.

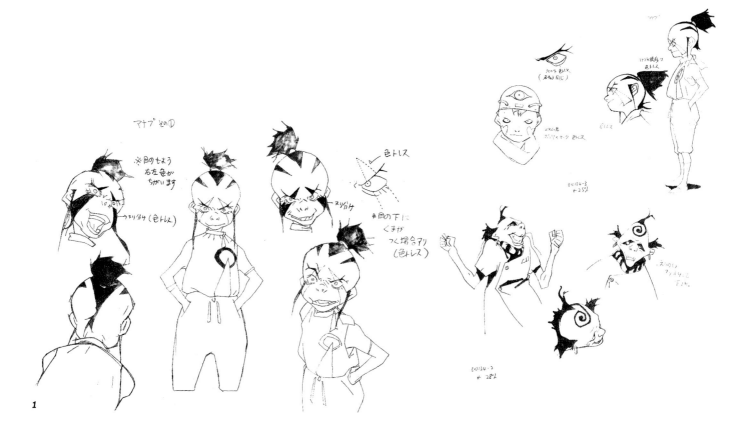

1

'I can't distinguish between my roles as animator and director, and I've been told that I lack the objectivity required of a director. I love drawing, and I have a hard time criticising others' work as well. People who don't draw might find it easy to put an artist's work down, but when I criticise I have to be ready to respond when my comment backfires and the artist replies, "OK, let's see you do it better!"' Morimoto never works nine to five since he doesn't feel his work to be simply a job, and he expects the same attitude from his staff, saying, 'This creates a strong bond, with everyone working in unison towards the same goal'.

Describing much of his work to date as 'surreal science-fiction', he has recently begun to move away from straight fantasy, focusing on what he calls different dimensions: 'The involvement of ordinary life with not so ordinary life, mixing the familiar and the unfamiliar. There are so many people who prefer to keep their eyes shut when an issue is close to their ordinary life. They will weep over refugees in a far country but consider the homeless people on their streets a menace.' Morimoto wants to explore such dichotomies. 'Because my experiences are limited, other people's opinions are very useful, especially when creating a piece that involves many different people. Socialising with people is my way of doing "research". When people drink, barriers between them come down, you can see beyond them, and it helps communication.'

Another new development is in his attitude to using dialogue. 'In the past, it was always the visuals which moved me emotionally, never words, so I tried to reduce dialogue to a minimum, and didn't put much effort into it. I thought using words showed a lack of confidence in what could be expressed pictorially.' The turning point was seeing Chaplin's anti-fascist talkie, **The Great Dictator**. He'd always been a fan of the actor and director's silents, but Chaplin's speech to Hitler in the film made him realise how important words were to him. As a result, he is now much more interested in using dialogue.

Apart from music promos, Morimoto has always added music to a finished piece, but is now considering putting the music first. 'Sometimes, even if the storyboard indicates a particular shot is 30 seconds, I find I would rather listen to the music for more than a minute, or allow myself to be lost in the music and not have to curtail my options. When the viewer's emotions become fully engaged, sometimes music is the only way to lead into a following effect. The directions a piece takes are often led or brought out by the music, especially when creating promos. So, maybe music should lead the way from the very start.'

(1) **Noiseman**: Character designs.

(2-4) **Extra**: A pop promo for Ken Ishii. Drawings, sketches and finished artwork.

(1–8) **Extra** was Morimoto's first foray into computer animation, and he worked with a team of 19 people for two months to create the four-minute film. He drew the pictures, but everything else – including painting and editing – was done on a Mac, using Form Z, Electric Image, and Astralworks software.

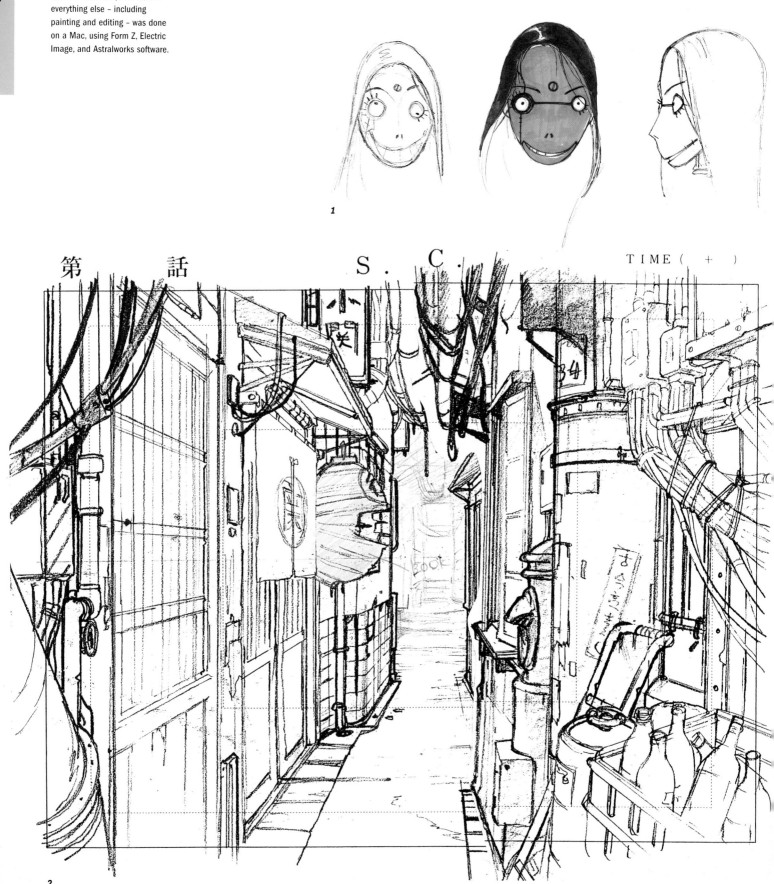

1

2

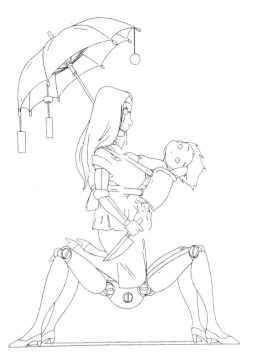

4

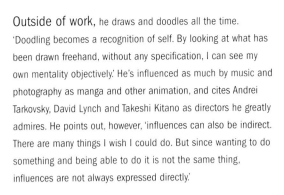

5

6

7

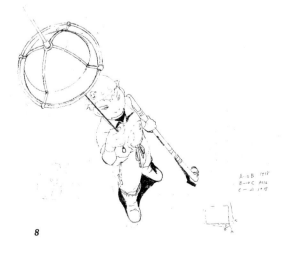

8

Outside of work, he draws and doodles all the time. 'Doodling becomes a recognition of self. By looking at what has been drawn freehand, without any specification, I can see my own mentality objectively.' He's influenced as much by music and photography as manga and other animation, and cites Andrei Tarkovsky, David Lynch and Takeshi Kitano as directors he greatly admires. He points out, however, 'influences can also be indirect. There are many things I wish I could do. But since wanting to do something and being able to do it is not the same thing, influences are not always expressed directly.'

Morimoto feels he can make no assumptions about his audience and although, 'I might pretend not to care too much, actually I care a lot. Opening day especially.' In addition to this, whilst having chosen animation as his form of expression – since 'pictures are my weapon and my passion' – he feels it is important to do other things, and enjoys DJ-ing: 'When you're making animation, you can't feel the audience's reactions, whereas as a DJ you do'.

He first used a computer to solve an animation problem on 'The Magnetic Rose' segment in **Memories**, but points out, 'computers don't do things by themselves, and using them doesn't change the manual creation of images'. He dislikes making a display of using computers, and sees their main advantage in speeding up the checking process. 'When animation was shot on film, it took a long time to be developed and printed, so checking, and doing any necessary re-takes was slower, and more time-consuming. Now, with computers, checks can be made almost simultaneously, whilst your tension is still high. A month or so later, it can be difficult to remember exactly what you had in mind, or you might lose the spark you had at the time.' The other advantage of computers, he adds, is that 'in the past, people without animation experience could not be involved in the industry, whereas now, if they're competent with a computer, and have interesting personalities, they can find a place in the industry. This widens the range of people you can work with. Even if someone was a bartender, we could probably work together.'

2

Folimage

The auteurs' studio

Folimage, a studio located in the provincial town of Valence in south-east France, has developed an enviable reputation for its ability to combine the production of innovative, quality TV children's entertainment with that of short, personal films. Whilst series production for TV might have been an economic necessity, it was also an organic development from the several years that studio founder Jacques-Rémy Girerd spent running animation workshops for children in schools, in parallel with his own filmmaking.

Although much of the studio's early output was plasticine animation, the range of techniques and styles has since evolved a great deal, and is now predominantly, although not exclusively, 2D. This development has also been fostered by the residency scheme Folimage initiated ten years ago, which has attracted talent to the studio from all over Europe, as well as Russia. Every year, two short film projects are selected from open submission, and the filmmakers spend eight months making their films at the studio with a crew drawn from Folimage staff. One beneficiary was Dutch animator Michaël Dudok de Wit, who had been working on commercials in the UK for over a decade, but could never secure finance for a personal film project – until his idea for **Le Moine et le Poisson** was accepted by Folimage. The film's international success enabled him to obtain finance for a second film.

Girerd sees the scheme as a way to support auteur filmmaking, and, just as importantly, to provide creative stimulus for the studio animators who benefit from new approaches and different techniques, to which they can also contribute. Further, the working relationships and skills thus developed can feed back into the studio's television productions, with de Witt, for example, working as an animator on their first major half-hour TV special, **L'Enfant au Grelot**.

Another, and increasingly productive spin-off benefit is the encouragement it offers Folimage animators to develop their own films, which can be scheduled in between work on studio productions. Breaking down the job/skill demarcations that are such a feature of industrialised animation production has clear advantages in terms of creative development. For studio animator Jean-Loup Felicioli, who had also made a number of shorts with plasticine, collaboration with Alain Gagnol led to a change of medium.

1

2

3

4

On top of their animator day jobs at Folimage, Gagnol was a published writer of detective thrillers, and Felicioli painted on the side. When Gagnol saw one of Felicioli's paintings, he felt their individual imaginative worlds could work well together. This led to **L'Egoiste**, a dark tale about a man whose narcissism knows no bounds. When a car accident leaves him facially disfigured, he can no longer bear the sight of the wife he'd loved for her resemblance to himself, and takes drastic action to save his marriage. As Felicioli began animating, they realised the film wouldn't work in plasticine, so switched to 2D, and the end result surprised them both. Felicioli was happy to discover he could abandon plasticine for a drawing style that was closer to his early fine-art training. The film's visual impact and unusual narrative tone prompted a commission for **Tragédies Minuscules**, a TV series of short, self-contained episodes for adult audiences. These brief, off-beat stories are innovative not only in content, but in their use of voiceover in relation to image.

Folimage's commercial productions have always been distinguished by their insistence on using 'real' children's voices (rather than the usual professional female voice artists used in most series and features) and a graphic style – for both characters and backgrounds – that is unlike conventional cartoon animation. Such distinctiveness led to a cinema release in France and Belgium for **L'Enfant au Grelot**, unusually for a half-hour TV programme. Its success, along with that of Michel Ocelot's feature film **Kirikou**, has enabled them to embark on their first feature film, **La Prophétie des Grenouilles**, a loose reworking of the Noah's Ark story.

5

(1–5) A sample of the range of styles and techniques used at Folimage: **(1)** Jean-Luc Greco and Catherine Buffat's **La Bouche Cousue**, using papier mâché characters and cardboard and papier mâché sets. **(2)** Iouri Tcherenkov's **La Grande Migration**, animated on tracing paper, paper and cel. **(3)** Michaël Dudok de Witt's **Le Moine et le Poisson**, using Indian ink, Chinese brushes, and watercolours. **(4)** Sarah Roper's **Le Chat d'Appartement**, drawn on cel and paper, using collage and rubber stamps. **(5)** Solveig von Kleist's **Le Roman de Mon Âme**, using acrylic paint on paper and cel.

1

5

6

(1–4) The series **Tragédies Minuscules**: *(1, 4)* Still and a storyboard extract from the episode 'A Knife amongst the Forks', in which a wife's misplaced piece of cutlery inspires murderous thoughts in her husband. *(2–3)* Stills from other episodes in the series. **L'Egoiste**'s style was simplified, refined and made lighter for the series, so as to concentrate more on character. The colouring also used less chalk, to avoid boiling. Felicioli and Gagnol storyboarded very quickly together, and then Felicioli enlarged each rough vignette, adding detail and developing the composition. Gagnol takes the drawings and determines keys, since, as Felicioli explains, 'the essence of the animation is contained within the drawings'.

(5) Sylain Vincendeau's **Paroles en l'Air**: Charcoal-accented drawings photocopied onto cel, painted and highlighted with chalk. *(6)* Konstantin Bronzit's **Au Bout du Monde**: Drawn on cel, and using collage. *(7–9)* Jacques-Rémy Girerd's **L'Enfant au Grelot**: Traditional drawn animation, coloured with oil pastel and paint.

2

3

(hidden behind a book, he watches her) (she walks past him)

(she's now walked past,
he leans over to keep her in sight)

(he gets up and follows her)

(he stops at the kitchen door)

(he watches her, remaining out of sight)

O.S.

O.S.

Could she have done it on purpose?

After all, a knife and fork are
nothing alike.

4

(she stretches out her hand)

(her hands moves towards the cutlery)

(he watches her intensely)

(her hand moves away from the
cutlery and turns the tap on)

(he slumps into his chair, defeated)

O.S.

She lies to me all the time,
wanting to make me think
she can't tell
a knife from a fork.

7

8

9

1

2

3

4

5

(1–6) The move from 3D to 2D in the production of **L'Egoiste**:
(1) Felicioli's painting sparked Gagnol's interest in collaboration on **L'Egoiste** and together they storyboarded Gagnol's script. Having used a rough drawn animatic as a guide for animating plasticine on his earlier solo shorts, Felicioli asked Gagnol to provide one for **L'Egoiste**. *(2–3)* Early plasticine maquettes. However, plasticine proved too thick and unwieldy to convey the painting's graphic qualities, nor was it fluid enough for the metamorphoses required. They realised the animatic's graphic style, drawn quickly as a rough guide, was in fact far better for the story. The stylised drawing also makes the violence less literal, *(4)* whilst animating the drawings on cel, then placing them on a glass sheet against 3D sets and backgrounds, retained a sense of volume. Gagnol's penchant for the dark and shocking was tempered by Felicioli's humour: for example, in the ending *(5)*, in which we see the couple grow old together. *(6)* A still from the finished animation.

(7–12) Developmental artwork demonstrating a rather different style for Gagnol and Felicioli's new project in development, **Le Nez à la Fenêtre**.

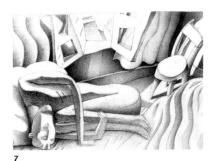

7

8

9   10

Girerd believes a combination of audacity and prudence
has helped the studio develop to its current position of strength.
Audacity, in terms of having the confidence to set themselves
new challenges and to break new ground; and prudence in
establishing a solid financial and artistic basis on which to
build. 'We've learned from everything we've done,' says Girerd:
'and waited for the studio to come of age before embarking
on the ambitious project to make a feature entirely within the
studio, rather than sending the animation abroad, since the
alchemy of a film, and its soul, is in the team behind it.'

The differences between feature and short filmmaking
are obvious in terms of sustaining a narrative, the commercial
investment and the management required for the exponential
rise in the work involved. Hence the standardised style and
production methods of so many animated features. Girerd
believes an auteur approach can be retained, drawing on the
experience gained from the cross-fertilisation of shorts and TV
productions, which has informed the development process.

11

12

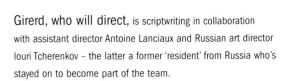

1

2

3

Girerd, who will direct, is scriptwriting in collaboration with assistant director Antoine Lanciaux and Russian art director Iouri Tcherenkov – the latter a former 'resident' from Russia who's stayed on to become part of the team.

As the storyboard was developing, so was work on colour design. Sensitive to the requirements of the cinema, as opposed to TV screen, they felt that a large-screen viewing of a cinema screening of the first rough storyboard – with some sequences in colour, and voices and sound effects recorded – would highlight any problems at an early stage. 'The rhythm of the colours is important. We found the transitions in some scenes were too dark, and this fed back into reworking the story's structure,' explains Girerd. Lanciaux adds that it also pinpointed storyboard problems, such as, 'how to visually translate "another day... then the next day" over three scenes that feature only three visual elements – the sea, the sky, and a boat – how to show time passing. Colour is a way to tell the story and to underscore its emotional resonance: it should be subliminal, although it is very consciously designed, with a great deal of discussion. The test also raised technical problems such as boiling: how to render chalk drawing for cinema-scale projection.'

(1–10) Work in progress from Folimage's first feature film **La Prophétie des Grenouilles**: (1–3) The earliest colour test drawings using ink and colour wash, with only a little chalk and colour pencil. Tcherenkov developed story ideas from embryonic ideas such as a sailor who is a musician, animals, and a Noah's Ark reference. (4) Rough sequence drawings.

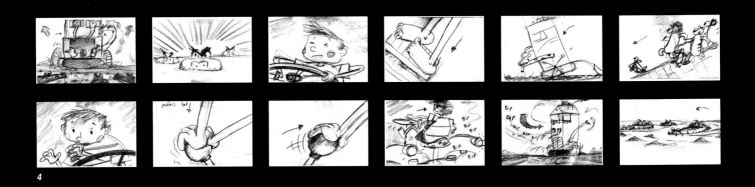

4

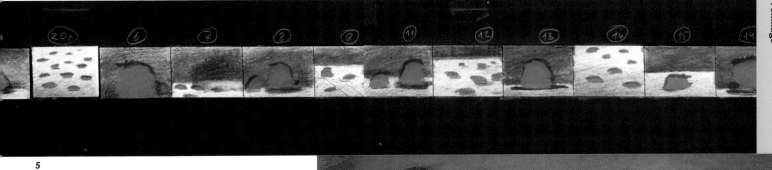

5

6

7

8

9

As the script developed, and in response to the test screenings, the drawings become more structured. *(7–8)* These images were used to illustrate a book Folimage had published to help raise finance. When the script and storyboard sequence seemed to hold together, Tcherenkov made small colour strips, concentrating not on the drawing, but purely on the colour *(5)*. Once the colour palette seemed right for a sequence, each drawn frame was enlarged and coloured to see how it worked, and further adjustments were made *(6)*. *(9–10)* The images soon became more stylised, with fewer colours.

10

(1–5) **La Prophétie des Grenouilles**: Drawings and illustrations from the book, and sketches for the film.

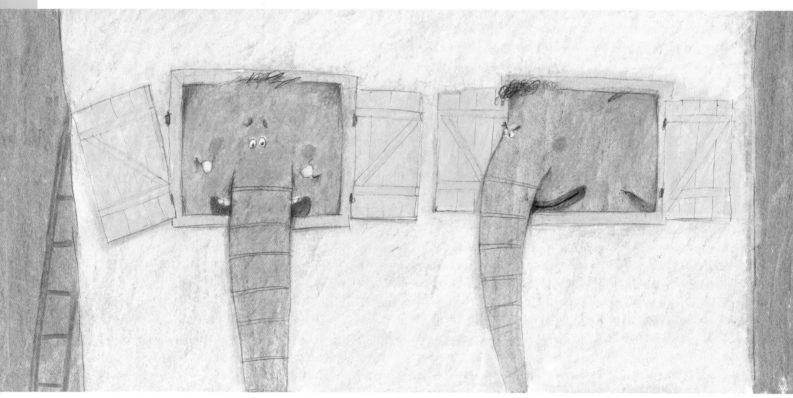

1

2

Most 2D feature films now rely heavily on computers. Until recently, Girerd observes, the available software was too crude and cartoon-like for what he sees as a Folimage hallmark: the textural use of chalk, oil pastels and paintbrush. 'Computers push you towards flat colour and no texture. This might have worked with a film like **Au Bout du Monde**, but otherwise it couldn't reproduce what we do by hand.' They are now testing computer capacity for achieving the textured effects they want by scanning drawings in monochrome, on various textured papers, then applying colour.

Girerd feels a real kinship with filmmakers such as Mark Baker, Paul Driessen, Fred Back and Miyazaki. 'Their work has an immediately recognisable graphic style, a fundamental sincerity, and a kind of simplicity which goes to the heart of things. Seeing how they have worked within limited budgets, retaining only the essential and exploiting the power of simplicity, has always inspired and encouraged us to continue in our own way.'

3

4

5

Filmographies

GIL ALKABETZ

Born 1957, Kibbutz Mashabei Sade, Israel. Studied at the Bezalel Academy of Art and Design, Jerusalem, Israel.

Filmography: 2000 **Lucky Stars** pilot film for TV series; 1998 **Kids Olympics** TV indent, Nickelodeon (Germany); 1997 **Rubicon** · 1st Prize, Animation Film, Filmvideo (Montecatini Terme, Italy) · Special Jury Prize, International Film Festival (Kelibia, Tunisia) · Jury Prize and Audience Prize, Castelli Animation Festival (Castelli Romani, Italy) · Best Animation Film, International Film Festival (Uppsala, Sweden) · Best Animation Film, Mediawave, International Festival of Visual Arts (Gyor, Hungary) · Best International Animation, Expo Cartoon (Rome, Italy) · Cappelletta d'Argento, Cappelletta d'Oro Film Festival (Alassio, Italy) · Silver Plaque, International Film Festival (Chicago, USA) · Funniest Film Award, International Animation Festival (Annecy, France); **Hands Off!** TV spot, ZDF (Germany); **Run Lola Run** title sequence; 1996 **Ecstazoo** · 3rd Prize, MTV Competition, Holland Animation Festival (Utrecht, the Netherlands) · 1st Prize, CARE Award Category, Promax Europe 1998; **Mice** commercial bumper, Nickelodeon (Germany); **Knights** commercial bumper, Nickelodeon (Germany); **How to Use a Tampon** TV spot, ZDF (Germany); **Can Opener Meets Can** TV spot, ZDF (Germany); 1995 **Yankale** · 1st Prize, Animation, International Short Film Festival (Krakow, Poland) · 1st Prize, Animation, Festival on Wheels (Ankara, Turkey) · International Jury Special Mention, Short Film Festival (Oberhausen, Germany) · Special Award, Film Certification Board (Wiesbaden, Germany) · Audience Prize, Mediawave, International Festival of Visual Arts (Gyor, Hungary) · Festival Prize, International Film Festival (Dresden, Germany) · International Film Critic Prize, Short Film Festival (Oberhausen, Germany) · Art Academy Students' Award, International Animation Festival (Zagreb, Croatia) · Special

Jury Prize, AnimExpo (Seoul, South Korea); **New TV World** TV indent, Nickelodeon (Germany); 1991 **Swamp** · 3rd Prize, International Animation Film Festival (Stuttgart, Germany) · Special Jury Prize, International Animation Festival (Ottowa, Canada) · Special Award, Film Certification Board (Wiesbaden, Germany) · Film Band in Gold, German Republic Short Film Event (Bonn, Germany); 1983 **Bitzbutz** · Best Animation, Israeli Cinema Institute Short Film Competition · (Tel Aviv, Israel) · 1st Prize, Veyrier Animation Film Festival (Geneva, Switzerland) · Special Jury Mention, International Animation Film Festival (Stuttgart, Germany)

NEVILLE ASTLEY

Born 1957, Keighley, Yorkshire, UK. Studied at Middlesex Polytechnic, London, UK.

Filmography: 1999 **The Big Knights** TV series, Co.Dir: Mark Baker · Best Adult Series, British Animation Awards (London, UK) · Most Creative Use of New Technologies, British Animation Awards (London, UK); 1996 **Trainspotter**, Co. Dir: Jeff Hewitt · Norman McLaren Award, Edinburgh Film Festival (Edinburgh, Scotland) · British Academy Award Nomination, British Academy of Film and Television Arts (London, UK) · Special Jury Prize, International Animation Festival (Hiroshima, Japan); 1989 **The Jump**; 1985 **Mobile Home**

MARK BAKER

Born 1959, London. Studied at the West Surrey College of Art and Design, UK then the National Film and Television School, Buckinghamshire, UK.

Filmography: 1999 **The Big Knights** TV series, Co.Dir: Neville Astley · Best Adult Series, British Animation Awards (London, UK) · Most Creative Use Of New Technologies, British Animation Awards (London, UK); **Jolly Roger** · Special Jury Award, International Animation Festival (Annecy, France) · Cartoon d'Or Nomination, European Association of Animated Film

(Brussels, Belgium) · British Academy Award Nomination, British Academy of Film and Television Arts (London, UK) · American Academy Award Nomination, Academy of Motion Picture Arts and Sciences (Los Angeles, USA); 1993 **The Village** · 1st Prize, International Short Film Festival (Krakow, Poland) · 1st Prize, Festival du Mons (Belgium) · 2nd Prize, International Animation Film Festival (Stuttgart, Germany) · Special Jury Prize, International Animation Festival (Annecy, France) · Best Short Film, Carrousel International Festival (Canada) · Best Television Film, International Animation Festival (Ottowa, Canada) · Hiroshima Prize, International Animation Festival (Hiroshima, Japan) · Silver Hugo Prize, International Film Festival (Chicago, USA) · American Academy Award Nomination, Academy of Motion Picture Arts and Sciences (Los Angeles, USA) · British Academy Award Nomination, British Academy of Film and Television Arts (London, UK) · Cartoon d'Or Nomination, European Association of Animated Film (Brussels, Belgium); 1988 **The Hill Farm** · 1st Prize, Film under Twenty Minutes, Cinanima International Animated Film Festival (Espinho, Portugal) · 2nd Grand Prize, International Animation Festival (Ottowa, Canada) · Grand Prize, International Animation Festival (Annecy, France) · Best Animation Film, International Film Festival (Sofia, Bulgaria) · Most Entertaining Film, International Film Festival (Munich, Germany) · Gold Plaque, International Film Festival (Chicago, USA) · Hiroshima Prize, International Animation Festival (Hiroshima, Japan) · British Academy Award, British Academy of Film and Television Arts (London, UK) · American Academy Award Nomination, Academy of Motion Picture Arts and Sciences (Los Angeles, USA); 1982 **The Three Knights** · Best Student Film, Cinanima International Animated Film Festival (Espinho, Portugal) · Silver Plaque, International Film Festival (Chicago, USA)

JOHN CARY

Born 1952, Kensington, London, UK.
Filmography: 2000 **Katya and the Nutcracker**;
Flash Boyfriend; 1998 **The Adventures of
Captain Pugwash** · Inde Award for Best
Animation, Carlton Producers' Alliance for
Cinema and Television (London, UK); 1994
William's Wish Wellingtons; 1993 **Rhinegold**;
1991 **Spider!**

FOLIMAGE

**Studio founded in 1984 by JAQUES-RÉMY
GIRERD, born 1952, Mars, France. Studied
at the College of Fine Art, Lyon, France.**
Studio Filmography: 1997 **L'Enfant au Grelot**
(The Child at the Bell or Charlie's Christmas)
Cartoon d'Or, European Association of
Animated Film (Brussels, Belgium) · Emmy
Award Nomination 1998 (New York, USA) · Best
TV Special, International Animation Festival
1998 (Annecy, France); 1996 **Ma Petite
Planète Chérie** (My Dear Little Planet) Unicef
Prize (Annecy, France) · Prize from the
Foundation of France (Paris, France); 1994
Mine de Rien (Quite Casually); 1992 **Le
Bonheur de la Vie** (The Joy of Life); 1990
Toujours Plus Vite (Quicker and Quicker);
1989 **Amerlock**; 1988 **La Rage du Desert**
(Desert Rage); 1986 **Le Petit Cirque de Toutes
les Couleurs** (The Little Multicoloured Circus);
1983 **Oshun**; 1982 **Pouce, on Tourne** (Turning
Thumb); 1980 **Rien de Special** (Nothing
Special); 1979 **D'une Gompa l'Autre** (From
One Gompa to Another); 1978 **Quatre Mille
Images Foetales** (Four Thousand Foetal
Images): all directed by Jaques-Rémy Girerd.
1995 **Paroles en l'air** (Words in the Air) direct-
ed by Sylain Vincendeau; 1996 **L'Egoiste** (The
Egoist) directed by Alain Gagnol and Jean-Loup
Felicioli; 1998 **La Bouche Cousue** (The
Stitched Mouth) directed by Jean-Luc Greco
and Catherine Buffat; 1994 **Le Moine et la
Poisson** (The Monk and the Fish) directed by
Michael Dudok de Wit; 1995 **La Grande**

Migration (The Big Migration) directed by Loi
Tcherenkov; 1997 **Le Roman de mon Ame**
(The Novel of my Soul) directed by Solweig von
Kleist; 1998 **Le Chat d'Appartment** (The
Appartment Cat) directed by Sarah Roper;
1999 **Au Bout du Monde** (At the End of the
World) directed by Konstantin Bronzit.

[The films listed in the Folimage filmography
are a multi-award-winning selection from
the studio's productions. As space limits
a comprehensive listing of prizes awarded,
further information can obtained from
Folimage@wanadoo.fr.]

AMANDA FORBIS

**Born 1963, Calgary, Alberta, Canada.
Studied at the Emily Carr College of Art
and Design, Vancouver, Canada.**
Filmography: 1999 **When the Day Breaks**,
Co-directed by Wendy Tilby (please refer to
Wendy Tilby's filmography for film's awards);
1995 **The Reluctant Deckhand**

DANIEL GREAVES

**Born 1959, Woburn, Buckinghamshire, UK.
Studied at the West Surrey College of Art
and Design, UK.**
Filmography: 1997 **Flatworld** · Jury Grand
Prize, Audience Prize, International Film Festival
(Hamburg, Germany) · Special International
Jury Prize, AnimExpo (Seoul, Korea) · Grand
Prize, Krok International Animation Festival
(Kiev, Ukraine) · Norman McLaren Award,
Edinburgh Film Festival (Edinburgh, UK) · Best
of Animation Prize, International Film Festival
(Vancouver, Canada) · Audience Prize,
International Film Festival (Leipzig, Germany)
· Audience Grand Prize, International Film
Festival (San Sebastián, Spain) · Audience
Prize, Cinanima International Animated Film
Festival (Espinho, Portugal) · Audience Prize,
International Film Festival (Regensburg,
Germany) · Audience Prize, International Film

Festival (Schorndorf, Germany) · Best Animation
for a TV Special, World Animation Celebration
(Los Angeles, USA) · 1st Prize, International
Film Festival (Ankara, Turkey) · 1st Prize,
International Short Film Festival (Krakow,
Poland) · Best Animated Programme,
Television Festival (Banff, Canada) · Jury Prize,
International Animation Festival (Zagreb,
Croatia) · Audience Prize, International
Animation Festival (Zagreb, Croatia) · Best
Animation, International Film Festival
(Melbourne, Australia) · Audience Prize,
International Film Festival (Matita, Italy); 1991
Manipulation · Mari Kuttna Award for Best
Newcomer, British Film Institute (London, UK)
· 1st Prize, Animated Short, International Film
Festival (Los Angeles, USA) · Special Jury Award
for Excellence, Cinanima International
Animated Film Festival (Espinho, Portugal)
· Gold Award for Best Animated Film,
International Film Festival (Bilbao, Spain) · 1st
Prize, Children's Category, International Film
Festival (Berlin, Germany) · American Academy
Award, Academy of Motion Picture Arts and
Sciences (Los Angeles, USA) · Cartoon d'Or,
European Association of Animated Film
(Brussels, Belgium) · Silver Plaque,
International Film Festival (Chicago, USA) ·
Cartoon Award (Treviso, Italy); 1996 **Rabbit
Rabbit**; 1988 **Family Tree**

PHILIP HUNT

**Born 1966, Bidcock-upon-Avon, UK.
Studied at Central St Martin's School of Art
then the Royal College of Art, London, UK.**
Filmography: 2000 **Time Magazine**; 1998
Perfect Coke commercial, Coca-Cola (USA);
1998/9 **Megalomaniac** commercial, Orange
(London, UK) · Craft Award, British Animation
Awards (London, UK) · Best Animation,
BTACA Silver (UK); **Hills, Reception, Words**
commercial, Orange (London, UK) · Best
Animation, BTACA (UK); 1996 **MTV European
Music Awards** title sequence · Monitor Award;

1995 **Reputations** TV title sequence; 1994 **Ah Pook is Here** · Best Film at the Cutting Edge, British Animation Awards (London, UK) · 1st Prize, International Film Festival (San Sebastián, Spain) · Silver Award, Expo of Short Film and Video (New York, USA) · 1st Prize, International Film Festival (Hamburg, Germany) · 1st Prize, International Film Festival (Dresden, Germany) · Jury Prize, Short Film Festival (Montreal, Canada) · Best Experimental Film, International Animation Festival (Ottawa, Canada) · Gold Plaque, International Film Festival (Chicago, USA) · Best Film in its Category, Cinanima International Animated Film Festival (Espinho, Portugal) · 1st Prize, Everyman Cinema Animation Awards (London, UK); 1991 **Spotless Dominoes**, Royal College of Art (London, UK) · Orsaca Prize, Best Graduating Student, Faculty of Communication · Mercedes Benz Kulturforderung Residency, Baden-Württemberg Film Academy, International Animation Film Festival (Stuttgart, Germany) · Bob Clampett Scholarship, World Animation Celebration (Los Angeles, USA) · 1st Prize, Student Film, International Animation Festival (Hiroshima, Japan); 1988 **The Beggar of the Dead Dog**

IGOR KOVALYOV

Born 1954, Kiev, Russia. Studied at the Film School, Moscow, Russia.

Filmography: 2000 **Flying Nansen** · Special Jury Prize, World Animation Celebration (Los Angeles, USA); 1998 **Rugrats** Co.Dir: Norton Virgien; 1996 **Bird in the Window** · Grand Prize, International Animation Festival (Ottawa, Canada) · Best Animation Short, Fantasy Film Festival (Sitges, Spain); 1993 **Aahh! Real Monsters** TV series · Originality Prize, International Animation Festival (Annecy, France) · Best Film in Category H, International Animation Festival 1994 (Ottawa, Canada); 1991 **Andrei Svislotsky** · Silver Dragon, 'Europa '92' Film Festival (Krakow, Poland) · Best

Experimental Film, Short Film Festival, (Oberhausen, Germany) · Best Film in its Category, Krok International Animation Festival (Kiev, Ukraine); 1989 **Hen, His Wife** · Grand Prize, and Best Film in its Category, International Animation Festival (Ottawa, Canada) · Special Jury Prize, International Animation Film Festival (Shanghai, China) · Best Film in its Category, Krok International Animation Festival (Kiev, Ukraine) · Selected for Competition, Cannes Film Festival (France)

PIET KROON

Born 1960, Baarn, the Netherlands. Studied Film and Theatre Studies at the University of Utrecht, the Netherlands.

Filmography: 2001 **Osmosis Jones** (animation co-director); 1997 **T.R.A.N.S.I.T** · Grand Prize, World Animation Celebration (Los Angeles, USA) · Best Animated Film in its Category, World Animation Celebration (Los Angeles, USA) · Shortlisted for American Academy Award Nomination, Academy of Motion Picture Arts and Sciences (Los Angeles, USA) · British Academy Award Nomination, Best Animated Short, British Academy of Film and Television Arts (London, UK) · Best Short Animated Film, Worldwide Short Film Festival (Toronto, Canada) · Cartoon d'Or Nomination, European Association of Animated Film 1998 (Brussels, Belgium) · Outstanding Achievement in an Animated Short Subject Nomination, 28th Annual Annie Awards ASIFA (California, USA) · Grand Prize 'Caixa Geral de Depositos', Cinanima International Animated Film Festival (Espinho, Portugal) · Audience Prize 'Nuno Lacerda Lopes', Cinanima International Animated Film Festival (Espinho, Portugal) · Best Short Animation, Los Angeles Film Critics' Awards 1998 (California, USA); 1994 **DaDA** · Spafax Airlines Special Award, Worldwide Short Film Festival (Toronto, Canada) · Golden Mikeldi for Best Animated Film, International Documentary and Short Film Festival (Bilbao,

Spain) · Special Jury Prize, Cinanima International Animated Film Festival (Espinho, Portugal) · Grand Prize for Best Short Film, Fantastic International Film Festival (Brussels, Belgium) · 2nd Prize for Best First Film, International Animation Festival (Zagreb, Croatia) · Public Award for Best Film, Anima Mundi Festival 1997 (Rio de Janeiro, Brazil); 1988 15 Years Holland Animation Festival leader; 1987 **The Balancer**

LEJF MARCUSSEN

Born 1936, Aabenraa, Jutland, Denmark. Studied at the Royal Academy of Arts, Copenhagen, Denmark.

Filmography: For all films: The Norman McLaren Heritage Award, for 'the uniqueness and originality of the body of work', International Animation Festival (Ottawa, Canada); 1992 **Lucifer**; 1988 **Den Offentlige Røst** (The Public Voice) · Special Distinction, International Animation Festival (Annecy, France) · Press Prize, International Animation Festival (Annecy, France) · Most Imaginative Film, International Film Festival (Odense, Denmark) · Best Essay, International Festival of Film Art (Montreal, Canada) · Best Animation, Nordic Short and Documentary Film Festival (Grimstad, Norway) · Best Camera Work, International Trickfilm Festival (Stuttgart, Germany) · Grand Prize, UNESCO International Festival of Film Art (Paris, France); 1983 **Tonespor** (Tonetrack); 1982 **Sten** (Stones): · **Ekko Fra Et Brev** (Echo from a Letter); 1979 **Maskedrifter** (Masks); **Stills**; 1977 **Et Billede** (A Picture); 1975 **Lederkonkurrence** (Master Competition); 1974 **Petrushka**; 1973 **En Kort Pause** (A Short Pause)

KOJI MORIMOTO

Born 1959, Wakayama-ken, Japan. Studied at the Osaka College of Designers, Japan.

Filmography: 1999 **Survival** music promo, Glay/Unlimited Records (Japan) · Prize for

Excellence, Non-Interactive Digital Art Section, 3rd Media Arts Festival (Tokyo, Japan); 1998 **Four Day Weekend** music promo, The Bluetones/A&M Records (England) · Grand Prize, Non-Interactive Digital Art Section, 2nd Media Arts Festival (Tokyo, Japan); 1997 **Noiseman Sound Insect** (Japan); 1996 **EXTRA** music promo, Ken Ishii/R&S Records (Japan); 1995 **Episode 1: Magnetic Rose** for Otomo's feature film, **Memories** (Japan) · Selected Feature Film, Japan Arts Fund (Tokyo, Japan); 1991 **Fly! Peak the Whale** (Japan); 1988 **Franken's Gears** (Japan)

MICHEL OCELOT

Born 1943, Villefranche-sur-Mer, France. Studied at the Institute for Decorative Arts, Paris, France then the Californian Institute for the Arts, USA.

Filmography: 1998 **Kirikou et la Sorcière** (Kirikou and the Sorceress) · Silver Trophy, Children's Film Festival (Cairo, Egypt) · Grand Prize, Feature Film, International Animation Festival (Annecy, France) · Grand Prize, Film Festival (Kecskmet, Hungary) · Audience Prize, International Film Festival (Zanzibar, Tanzania) · Feature Film Prize, Cinanima International Animated Film Festival (Espinho, Portugal) · Feature Film Prize, Children's Film Festival (Sousse, Tunisia) · Feature Film Prize, Krok International Animation Festival (Kiev, Ukraine) · Adult and Children's Jury Prize, Children's Film Festival (Chicago, USA) · Best Film for Children Prize, Film Festival (Rouyn-Noranda, Canada) · Feature Film Prize, Film Festival (Oulu, Finland) · Special Jury Prize, Children's Film Festival (Montreal, Canada) · Best Feature Prize, Film Festival (Malmô, Finland) · Children's Jury Prize, International Film Festival (Vancouver, Canada); 1992 **Les Contes de la Nuit** (Tales of the Night) TV special (Trilogy: **La Belle Fille et le Sorcier** 'The Pretty Girl and the Sorcerer'; **Bergère qui Danse** 'The Dancing Sheperdess'; **Le Prince des Joyaux** 'The Prince

of Jewels'); 1989 **Cíne Si** (**La Princesse des Diamants** 'The Princess of the Diamonds'; **Le Garçon des Figues** 'The Fig Boy'; **La Reine Cruelle** 'The Cruel Queen'; **La Sorcière** 'The Sorceress'; **Princes et Princesses** 'The Princes and Princesses'; **Icare** 'Icarus'; **On ne Saurait Penser à Tout** 'You Can't Think of Everything'; **Le Manteau de la Vieille Dame** 'The Old Woman's Coat') · César Nomination, Academy of Arts and Cinema Techniques (Paris, France) · Best Children's Programme, International Animation Festival (Ottawa, Canada); 1987 **Les Quatre Voeux** (The Four Wishes) · Selected for Competition, Cannes Film Festival (France); 1986 **La Princesse Insensible** (The Insensitive Princess), 13 Episodes · 1st Prize, Film Festival (Bourg-en-Bresse, France) · Audience Prize, International Film Festival (Odense, Denmark); 1982 **Beyond Oil**; **La Légende du Pauvre Bossu** (The Legend of the Poor Hunchback); 1981 **Les Filles de l'Égalité** (The Daughters of Equality); 1979 **Les Trois Inventeurs** (The Three Inventors) · British Academy Award, British Academy of Film and Television Arts (London, UK) · 1st Prize, International Animation Festival (Zagreb, Croatia) · César Nomination, Academy of Arts and Cinema Techniques (Paris, France) · Gold Trophy, International Film Festival (Odense, Denmark); 1976 **Gedeon**, 60 Episodes; 1974 **Le Tabac** (The Newsagent)

PRIIT PÄRN

Born 1946, Tallinn, Estonia. Studied Biology at the University of Tartu, Estonia.

Filmography: 1998 **The Night of the Carrots** · Grand Prize, International Animation Festival (Ottawa, Canada) · Grand Prize, World Animation Celebration (Los Angeles, USA) · Grand Prize, International Animation Festival (Ottawa, Canada); 1996 **Absolut Pärn** internet animation · Best Campaign, Holland Animation Film Festival (Utrecht, the Netherlands) · Diploma, Krok International Animation Festival

(Kiev, Ukraine); 1995 **Deliss** commercial; **1895** Co.Dir: Janno Poldma · 3rd Youth Jury Prize, International Film Festival (Odense, Denmark) · Critics' Award of ASIFA Russia, Krok International Animation Festival (Kiev, Ukraine) · Best Film in Category C, Cinanima International Animated Film Festival (Espinho, Portugal) · Grand Prize, International Film Festival (Oslo, Norway) · Grand Prize and Critics' Award, International Animation Festival (Zagreb, Croatia); 1992 **Hotel E** · Baden-Württemberg Prize, International Animation Film Festival (Stuttgart, Germany); 1988 **Switch off the Lights** commercial · Bronze Lion, Cannes Advertising Festival (France); 1987 **Breakfast on the Grass** (aka Luncheon on the Grass) · Grand Prize, Film Festival (Tampere, Finland) · Grand Prize and Critics' Award, International Animation Festival (Zagreb, Croatia) · Grand Prize, Cinanima International Animated Film Festival (Espinho, Portugal) · 1st Prize, International Animation Festival (Shanghai, China) · 1st Prize, Film Festival (Russia) · Best Animated Film, Short Film Festival (Melbourne, Australia) · NIKA Academy Award 1989, Soviet Academy of Film (Russia) · 3rd Prize, International Film Festival (Odense, Denmark); 1984 **Time Out** · Grand Prize, International Film Festival (Varna, Bulgaria) · 1st Prize, Cinanima International Animated Film Festival (Espinho, Portugal) · Best Animated Film, International Documentary and Short Film Festival (Bilbao, Spain); 1980 **Exercises for an Independent Life** · 2nd Prize, Triangle, Film Festival 1982 (Russia); 1978 **And Now Play Tricks** · Best Children's Film, International Film Festival (Varna, Bulgaria); 1977 **Is the Earth Round?**

SIMON PUMMELL

Born 1959, Norwich, UK. Studied English Literature at Oxford University, UK then Film at the Royal College of Art, London, UK.

Filmography: 2000 **Blinded by Light**; 1998 **Ray Gun Fun**; 1995 **Evolution**; **Heart-Ache**;

Digital Baby; **Butcher's Hook** · Most Creative
Use of New Technologies, British Animation
Awards (London, UK); 1994 **Rose Red**; 1993
The Temptation of Sainthood · Main Prize,
Short Film Festival (Oberhausen, Germany) ·
Special Prize, Mediopolis Video Festival 1994
(Berlin, Germany) · Best Short, International
Film Festival 1994 (Fantasporto, Portugal);
British Film Institute 1992-93 Corporate Video
(London, UK); 1992 **Cupid**; **Stain**; 1991 **The
Secret Joy of Falling Angels** · Grand Prize, Short
Film Festival 1992 (Oberhausen, Germany) ·
Best Experimental Film, International Animation
Film Festival 1992 (Stuttgart, Germany); 1986
Surface Tension · Mari Kuttna Award for Most
Original New Animated Film, British Film
Institute (London, UK)

WENDY TILBY
**Born 1960, Edmonton, Canada. Studied at
the University of Victoria, Canada then the
Emily Carr College of Art and Design,
Vancouver, Canada.**
Filmography: 1999 **When the Day Breaks**,
Co.Dir: Amanda Forbis · Palme d'Or, Cannes
Film Festival (France) · Grand Prize,
International Animation Festival (Annecy,
France) · Grand Prize, International Film Festival
(Leipzig, Germany) · Golden Spire Award,
International Film Festival (San Francisco, USA)
· Grand Prize, Worldfest, International Film
Festival (Houston, USA) · Bronze World Medal,
International Film and Video Festival (New York,
USA) · Genie Award, Academy of Canadian
Cinema and Television (Toronto, Canada)
· Best Film, Cinanima International Animated
Film Festival (Espinho, Portugal) · Gold Hugo
Award, International Film Festival (Chicago,
USA) · American Academy Award Nomination,
Academy of Motion Picture Arts and Sciences
(Los Angeles, USA) · Grand Prize, International
Animation Festival (Hiroshima, Japan) ·
Director's Choice Award, Black Maria Film and
Video Festival (New Jersey, USA); 1991 **Strings**

· Genie Award, Academy of Canadian Cinema
and Television (Toronto, Canada) · 1st Prize
(ex-aequo), Cinanima International Animated
Film Festival (Espinho, Portugal) · 1st Prize, Expo
of Short Film and Video (New York, USA) · Press
Prize, International Animation Festival (Annecy,
France) · 1st Prize, International Animation
Festival (Hiroshima, Japan) · Oscar Nominee,
American Film and Video Festival (USA); 1986
Tables of Content · 1st Prize, International
Animation Festival (Ottawa, Canada) · 1st Prize,
(debut category), International Animation
Festival (Shanghai, China) · 1st Prize, (debut
category), Cinanima International Animated
Film Festival (Espinho, Portugal) · Genie Award
Nomination, Academy of Canadian Cinema and
Television (Canada) · Grand Prize for Short Film,
World Film Festival (Montreal, Canada)

Glossary

Anticipation A technical animation term meaning the precursor to an animated character's movement, in which the same character is made to move slightly in the opposite direction. This accentuates the move itself and creates more flourish and exaggeration than is found in the naturalistic equivalent move made by an actor.

Cel A thin (120 micron), transparent, acetate sheet (the same material as photographic film) onto which the animator's character drawings are traced in ink. Paint is applied on the reverse side, and viewed through the cel level (to create the smoothest effect). Since the characters are surrounded by a transparent layer, other layers and the background can be seen clearly through the cel levels, although it becomes impractical to exceed eight levels.

Colour model A cel painting or computer-painted master colour guide for use by cel painters or computer colourists. The same system applies to digital painting, except the guide is created on the computer and can include a range of alternative palettes for different lighting conditions (day, night, sunset, interior or exterior).

Compositing The digital computer equivalent of rostrum photography. Each scanned layer is placed in the correct order according to the dope sheet, and scaled according to the layout. Camera instructions and field keys (framing sizes) are also read from the dope sheet.

Construction sketches/construction drawings A drawing breaking a character down into elementary geometrical volumes (either ellipsoids or cuboids), showing proportion, joints and attitude, but no detail.

Digital ink and paint The computerised form of 'trace and paint' (although the old terms are still used). The animator's drawings are scanned into the computer system (there are about four different rival systems worldwide), after which the colour is applied on screen. Computer systems allow much greater flexibility than the traditional methods, particularly when effecting changes and amendments. The painter can use a range of electronic 'palettes' created for each character which will remain absolutely constant throughout a film or series.

Dingles Term used by film electricians for odd shapes made from card or metal, suspended in front of the film lights to create interesting shadow shapes which fall across the scene. In the context used in this book, the term has been adapted, by John Cary Studios, to mean props and pieces of scenery moved into shot in semi-silhouette, to re-create the film frame and give the viewer a sense of depth and peering round objects to see the scene.

Dissolve-free zone The 'dissolve' is often referred to as a 'mix' in animation and is the blending of two scenes over a short time so that one appears to emerge out of the other. A very short dissolve is known as a 'soft cut'. The device was used frequently in older films to signal a substantial time or space break to the audience (e.g. 'Two hours later', or 'Meanwhile in Paris') – a very large break would be shown by using a fade out to black and fade in. Modern audiences are much more familiar with film language, and now accept time and space breaks much more readily, so some animators prefer to use more efficient ways of showing the passing of time, like a sharp cut to close-up, a definite change of background sound effects, or a music cue.

Dope sheet/exposure sheet The basic 'score' fundamental to the timing of the drawing sequences. Arranged in vertical columns, it shows the rostrum camera operator or computer compositor which drawings to use on which level, on which frame (exposure), what framing (field keys) and where to move the camera (pans and tracks).

Filmic picture plane The virtual surface onto which a photographed image would be placed from the viewpoint of the camera. The term is used when creating extreme optical illusions such as those created by painting part of a scene on glass which matches in with a real scene. The glass would have to be placed in the exact film picture plane in order to match perspectives with the camera viewpoint.

Fine cut The final assembly of all shots in the completed film, trimmed to their exact length and assembled in the exact order in which they will appear in the final print or master video tape. The process is the last of the picture editing stages (after rough assembly, assembly, and rough cut). However, in animation there is no spare footage or shots, so the fine cut is often the final polish after assembling the rushes. Even after colour animation, there are a few opportunities to insert new shots, invert or move shots and trim shots.

Flying logos A term, often used derogatorily, applying to computer generated lettering and logos which can be easily manipulated to 'fly' into and across the screen, often using flashy silver or glass textures in a hyper-real way. The technique is commonly used by film distributors and exhibitors for screen presentation and for news and current affairs programmes.

In-betweener (often synonymous with animation assistant) The artist who draws the interval drawings between key poses. These drawings create the illusion of seamless, continuous movement.

Key poses (key drawings/keys) The main poses and positions of the characters, in their most extreme positions. These drawings will be 'in-betweened' (i.e. linked by interval drawings) by the animation assistant or in-betweener – e.g. key 1: character sitting back in chair, key 2: leaning back in anticipation of upward move, key 3: extreme standing position, key 4: end pose resting at standing position.

Layout Two registered drawings showing at bottom level the full background drawing, (including lines which characters will go behind or interact with), and at top level, all the characters in their opening and closing poses in the shot. From this drawing (the layout) which is done by a layout artist, the animator takes all his/her start-point information.

Line producer A term generally used in film and TV production to denote a hired-in 'producer' who occupies the same position as the production manager with a more elevated title. The line producer is paid a fee and does not have any financial interest in the film.

Line tests/pencil tests The animator's raw pencil drawings registered one to the other, recorded one frame at a time and pegged onto a video camera system using hard disk or tape. This process is often synchronised with the dialogue to check lip-synchronisation, the animation line, kinetics, timing and poses, prior to 'trace and paint'.

Manga Japanese cartoon strip storytelling i.e. print media, although the term is often used to describe Japanese animated films.

Model sheet Very accurate engineering drawings of all characters showing the animators exactly how to draw the character in every position (front, profile, back, 3/4, and back 3/4). Detailed model sheets show facial detail, lip positions for each phonetic unit and a range of emotional expressions. This ensures that any number of animators (sometimes up to a hundred), will draw the character consistently and preserve the essential personality.

Non-linear (digital) media (1) To mean non-linear editing: A general term used to describe proprietary computer-editing systems such as Avid and Speed-Razor. Old-fashioned video tape 'linear' editing relied on piling one trimmed shot onto another – if the editor wanted to go back and revise an earlier sequence after completing the edit, all the edits after that revision needed to be updated and re-compiled. Although computer-controlled tape edit suites did a lot to alleviate this problem, most traditional film editors hated this system which was non-intuitive and clumsy. The introduction of the non-linear systems meant editors could once again enjoy all the benefits of film editing without having to deal with physical film or tape joiners. All the iconography in non-linear systems is based on film editing tradition, including on-screen bins for rushes and trims.

Non-linear (digital) media (2) To mean non-linear audio-visual programme making: The advent of CD Rom and the internet has meant that audio-visual material no longer needs to run in a pre-determined sequence (as conventional TV or film programming does). The viewer is able to select pieces or sections of audio-visual material (often an animation clip with sound) from the available body of material and play the sections in any sequence, or a sequence that is determined through choice or another interactive device. Although this method of presentation flies in the face of conventional narrative technique (the author is unable to lead you through a story as he/she would like), it is used extensively in education and training presentations. The material is normally accessed through a master map or guide, and the CD Rom author can delimit the viewer's choice in all sorts of ways buried in the computer code. The classic use is in an adventure game where the player is confronted with multiple choices at every turn of the plot, and can twist the story (and the outcome) according to his or her skill.

Render (1) Crayoning: Using traditional cel-based animation, a special frosted (roughened) cel is employed, onto which the drawings are traced and painted on the back in the normal way. This is then turned back to the facing side and crayon or wax pencil is applied on the roughened surface to produce coloured-on monotone modelling and shadow tones. The best known film to use this is **The Snowman**. The Beatrix Potter series also used it extensively to create the effect of fur, feathers and other textures.

Render (2) The final calculations a computer makes to produce the actual image which will be transferred to digital tape or film. During the process of creating the computer shot or composition, the computer produces low-resolution images on screen to check and revise – after the shot is approved it is set to render the scene (a process often done overnight while the computer is otherwise idle) at full TV (768 x 576 pixels) or film resolution (1536 x 1152 pixels). A series of high quality TIFFs or TGAs (or other picture file format) are produced ready to be translated to PAL or NTSC TV formats or to go straight to the 35mm film recorder which burns the image onto the film using coloured lasers.

Rostrum camera A film or video camera fixed on a moveable 'truck' pointing vertically down onto a table, the rostrum. The whole assembly is known as a rostrum camera stand. The table moves on threaded bars (to an accuracy of 1/1000 inch) to create horizontal (east/west) and vertical (north/south) pans and the camera truck moves up and down on a column to create tracks in or out (called 'trucks' in the US, but the equivalent of a zoom on a film camera). The cels and backgrounds are registered to the table by means of pegs which match the animator's pegs exactly. Stands use computer-controlled servo motors, and a video camera viewfinder enables the operator to see the frames as they are exposed.

Rushes/dailies The raw film shots, printed in colour, synchronised with the dialogue track. A general term in the film industry which derives from the way film laboratories work. The exposed negative is sent to the lab at the close of the day, for processing and printing overnight. By eight a.m. the colour print is ready for viewing by the production crew before starting to film again the next day (an overnight 'rush' print – viewed on a 'daily' basis), ensuring that technical and continuity errors are spotted before the 'actors' are released and the 'set' struck. The term is used generally to denote the raw film print or digital tape of the composited work, not in sequence order, which is ready to be checked and edited together.

Scene In animation, scene is synonymous with 'shot', but can be confusing since scriptwriters use the term 'scene' in the theatrical sense meaning an action and dialogue sequence in unified space and time.

Stop-motion animation Generally applied to filming model puppet or plasticine animated films, but is also applied to pixelation (the movement of real people in an animated way). The moving image is produced by filming successive still images frame-by-frame, using a specially adapted film camera, so that when projected at normal speed of 24 fps (frames per second), inanimate objects appear to move spontaneously.

Storyboard A pictorial rendition of the script or scenario, normally showing one panel per shot of the final film. Apart from the dialogue recording, the storyboard replaces the script as the master basis for the animated film, indicating character poses, composition, camera angle, dialogue text, special effects, camera moves, continuity and timing. The storyboard is often filmed and synchronised with the dialogue soundtrack to produce an animatic or Leica reel. Storyboards are now commonly used by live-action filmmakers to plan action sequences.

Straight-ahead animation Traditional drawn animation uses the key/in-between method, so that an animator can pre-determine the finish point of an animation move, check that it works and then work out the intervals. Straight-ahead animation relies on the animator's intuitive sense of place, timing and kinetics to ensure a character finishes on a given mark (as would a real actor). In fact, it is the accidental nature of this system which excites the animators who use it, since it is much higher risk but more 'natural'. In model animation, since there is no opportunity for keys and in-betweens, straight-ahead is always used. The mental 'trick' is to imagine the entire scene in motion all the time – thus the placing of the model fits into a pre-determined move in the animator's head. This takes years of experience and a substantial amount of natural flair.

3D shots Shots generated using a 3D animation computer program such as Lightwave, 3D Studio Max, Maya or similar systems. In these systems, a virtual 3D 'stage' is created, objects placed on the stage, with the camera and lights able to move freely around the stage and objects. The objects can be created using 2D and placed in the 3D scene, or the objects can be created using the computer's own modelling system, where the modeller sculpts or builds characters or scenery. The objects can be animated either by 2D animation – a sequence of 2D coloured drawings, replaced a frame at a time, or by 3D animation – the 3D objects can be animated and moved using computer calculations much in the way that models are manipulated on a model stage.

Trace and paint/Ink and paint The process of tracing animators' drawings (keys and in-betweens) onto cel in ink, reversing the cel and painting the colours in on the back using a vinyl-based paint which is flexible and not prone to cracking. Colours have to be mixed by hand for each area of the character and consistency maintained throughout production. The 'ink-and-painter' is the person who performs these tasks. Now this task is generally done on a computer and is referred to as 'digital ink and paint': a colourist or digital painter being the person who performs this.

Virtual zoom A zoom lens created in the computer; programs like Lightwave have a full virtual camera, with interchangeable lenses, and zooms calibrated in millimetre focal lengths (for 35mm movie cameras) to match real zoom lenses. Animators can begin on a 25mm wide-angle focal length lens and zoom into a 250mm telephoto, framing as they would on a normal zoom lens of the ratio ten to one.

Index

Credits and acknowledgements

From shorts to series production: p 10–19 Visual material contributed by Neville Astley and Mark Baker; with thanks and acknowledgement to BBC Worldwide Ltd. 2000 TM BBC/The Big Knights Ltd. for p 12–13 (1–12) and p 18–19 (5–10); with thanks and acknowledgement to Channel Four Television Corporation 1999 for p 18–19 (1–4).

Series production: p 20–27 Visual material contributed by John Cary, with thanks and acknowledgement to © Gullane (Development) Ltd. 2000 for p 20 (1), p 22–23 (3, 6–9), p 24–25 (1–8) and p 26–27 (3–5), with thanks and acknowledgement to John Ryan/Penguin Books Ltd. 2000 for p 20–21 (2), p 22–23 (2), with thanks and acknowledgement to John Ryan/Random house Group Ltd. For p 21 (3, 7), p 23 (1), with thanks and acknowledgement to John Ryan 2000 for p 21 (4–6), p 22–23 (5), with thanks and acknowledgement to the National Railway Museum/Science & Society for p 22 (4), with thanks and acknowledgement to the City of Prague Philharmonic for p 26 (1), with thanks and acknowledgement to composer Ian Nicholls, © Gullane (Development) Ltd. 2000 for p 26 (2).

Advanced production techniques: p 28–37 Visual material contributed by Simon Pummell; with thanks and acknowledgement to Koninck Projects/C4 for p28–29 (1–5), p30 (3–5), p32 (1), p33 (2), with thanks and acknowledgement to Koninck Projects/British Film Institute for p31 (9), with thanks and acknowledgement to Finetake/Hot Property for p34 (1), p35 (2), p36 (1–2), p37 (3), with thanks and acknowledgement to Nikon UK for p35 (3), with thanks and acknowledgement to photographer John McMurtrie p 35.

Focusing on form: p 38–47 Visual material contributed by Gil Alkabetz.

From 3D to 2D: p 48–57 Visual material contributed by Philip Hunt.

Collaborative filmmaking: p 58–67 Visual material contributed by Wendy Tilby, with thanks and acknowledgement to The National Film Board of Canada for all images on p 58–67 excluding p 48 (1–2).

From Russia to Hollywood: p 68–75 Visual material contributed by Igor Kovalyov.

Exploring visual ambiguity: p 76–87 Visual material contributed by Lejf Marcussen.

Processing the creative thought: p 88–99 Visual material contributed by Piet Kroon; with thanks and acknowledgement to © Cilia van Dijk Film productions, the Netherlands/Picture Start Animations, the Netherlands, for p 90 (3–6), with thanks and acknowledgement to © Pieter Hoogenbirk, Comic House for p 90 (7–8), with thanks and acknowledgement to Illuminated Film Company Ltd., UK for © p 91 (1–9), p 96–97 (2, 4–5), p 99 (5–6), with thanks and acknowledgement to the Seaco Picture Library for p 97 (5).

The storyteller: p 100–109 Visual material contributed by Michel Ocelot; with thanks and acknowledgement to les amateurs/Odec Kid Cartoons/Exposure/TEF/Monipoly/France 3 cinéma for p 106–107 (1–11), p 108–109 (1–11).

Engineering narrative: p 110–119 Visual material contributed by Priit Pärn as follows: graphic design, p 110–111 (1–6), p 112–113 (3–4, 9), p 114–115 (2–3, 5–7), p 116–117 (2–8), p 118–119 (1–6, 10), drawings, p 112–113 (1–2, 6,10), p 114–115 (1, 4, 8), p116–117 (1), p 118–119 (8–9, 11), etchings, p 118–119 (12–13), charcoal drawing, p 118–119 (14). With thanks and acknowledgement to Svetlana Saks, colourist for p 110–111 (1–2), with thanks and acknowledgement to Miljard Kilk, colourist for p 112–113 (3–4, 9) p 114–115 (2–3, 5–7), p 116–117 (2–8), p 118–119 (1–6, 10), and painter of p 112–113 (7, 8).

Exploring different techniques: p 120–129 Visual material contributed by Daniel Greaves; with thanks and acknowledgement to British Airways and M+C Saatchi for p 128 (1), with thanks and acknowledgement to Schweppes and BMP DDB Needham for p 128 (2), with thanks and acknowledgement to Tesco and Lowe Lintas for p 128 (3), with thanks and acknowledgement to Hellmann's and Grey World Wide for p 128 (4), with thanks and acknowledgement to Very Fine Apple Quenchers and Mullen's, Boston, USA for p 129 (6).

A high tension approach: p 130–139 Visual material contributed by Moji Morimoto; with thanks and acknowledgement to © Unlimited Records for p 130 (1–2), with thanks and acknowledgement to © Beyond C./Bandai Visual for p 133 (8), with thanks and acknowledgement to © R&S Records/Beyond C. for p 139 (1–2).

The auteurs' studio: p 140–149 Visual material contributed by Patrick Eveno at Folimage-Valence-Production; with thanks and acknowledgement to Jacques-Remy Girerd for p 140.

Thank you to John Ryan, the original author of Captain Pugwash; Random House Books; Penguin Books; BBC Television, the broadcaster of the original Captain Pugwash series; Gullane Entertainment, the copyright owners of the new **Adventures of Captain Pugwash**; Philip Pepper, designer of 'Jonah' and first animation director of the new **Adventures of Captain Pugwash**; Dorse Jukes, the colour and style designer for the new **Adventures of Captain Pugwash**; Alastair Graham, production designer of the new **Adventures of Captain Pugwash**; Mich Harper, the computer animator of the new **Adventures of Captain Pugwash**; and Colin White, the supervising director for the new **Adventures of Captain Pugwash**. The National Film Board of Canada as the producers of **Strings** and **When the Day Breaks**. Sue Goffe, Pam Oennis, Mario Cavalli and the directors, designers and staff at Studio AKA. Dr-TV for **Tonnespor** and **The Public Voice**. Iain Harvey, Cecile Wijne, Gill Bradley and Cilia van Dijk, Marcelle Ponti, aaa, producer of **Les Trois Inventeurs**; Christian Maire, composer of the music for **Les Trois Inventeurs**; Jean-François Laguionie, La Fabrique, the producer of **CINE SI**, latterly called **Princes et Princesses**; Didier Brunner, Les Armateurs, the producer of **Kirikou et la Sorcière**; Odec-Kid-Cartoon, Monipoly and Studio O, the co-producers of **Kirikou et la Sorcière**; and Youssou N'Dour, the composer of the music for **Kirikou et la Sorcière**. Tandem films, Geraldine Barnedes for the documentation and all the directors of Folimage.

Thanks also to Jean-Pierre Barja, John Cary, Darren Wall, Alex Jennings, Gill Bradley, Iain Harvey, Ian McCue; Nurit Israeli, Gabor Csupo, Marisa Materna, Terry Thoren at Klasky Csupo; Nexus: Charlotte Lambert, Julia Parfitt, Chris O'Reilly, Shigeto Sayama and Mamiko in Japan. Claire Jennings, Sarah Lutton, London Film Festival, les Armateurs, Paris; Patrick Eveno and Antoine Lanciaux, Folimage; Lenny Borger, Andreas Hykade, Ged Haney, and Matthew Snead at Automatic Television; Mireille Roulet in France, Jane Taylor at the National Film Board of Canada in London and Hélène Tanguy at the National Film Board of Canada, Montréal; Luke Mitchell and Erica Ffrench at RotoVision and Dean Koonjul.